Debbie~

The Heart
of a
Warrior

Praying you enjoy the journey through these pages!
God Bless~
Kim Rice Smith

Kim Rice Smith

ISBN 978-1-64458-696-9 (paperback)
ISBN 978-1-64492-290-3 (hardcover)
ISBN 978-1-64458-697-6 (digital)

Christian Faith Publishing, Inc.
832 Park Avenue
Meadville, PA 16335
www.christianfaithpublishing.com

Printed in the United States of America

Dedication

This book is dedicated to a beautiful Warrior, Donia Rene Cotton. Donia passed away on September 19, 2018, after a hard fought battle with colon cancer.

During her illness, she taught the rest of us how to live. Donia laughed up until her last minutes on this earth. She loved everyone, with everything she had. Donia pulled a group of very different women together with her heart as our common denominator. She showed us how to love unconditionally. She taught us how to laugh through the pain.

Donia helped us all witness absolute faith and grace. She helped me personally, grow in my journey of faith. She was a force to be reckoned with as she fought for those she loved. Her faith…unshakeable. Donia was a warrior in her battle with cancer. More importantly, she lived her entire life with the fierce heart of a loving warrior.

Crumbling Walls

I often ride by this abandoned house that looks like it could crumble at any moment. Some windows have been boarded up, and ropes guard access to it and discourage unsafe exploration.

When I look at it, my mind wanders to the lives of those who once laughed and cried within those walls. I imagine children playing in the front yard. I see beauty in what some would prefer be torn down.

If you look closely, you can see trees and shrubs growing from within this crumbling structure—new growth and life coming from decay.

This house has survived hurricanes and historic floods. It is not standing nearly as strong as it once did, but it is still standing—almost as if to remind those who drive by, "My story is not complete." This house has much to say.

Aging can be a really beautiful thing depending on your viewpoint and attitude. I have seen people work through illness and financial struggles with tremendous dignity and beauty. I often wonder how they find the strength in this life amidst such struggles. Would I be that strong? Could I smile through the pain?

Then I will ride by this structure, and I am reminded that even when things are falling apart, there is profound beauty. Even though my body feels like it may be crumbling some days, my story is not complete. God isn't done with me just yet—or with you!

If you are hurting and struggling and wondering how much longer you can hold on—think of this house. Some of the strongest people I know probably feel like this house every once in a while. But I see their strength, their beauty, and their hearts when I am in their presence.

Just as every crack in the wall of this structure tells a story, so does every achy bone on my body and yours. Oh, the stories that house and we all could tell! Those stories that we need to share with each other are how new life begins to grow from our own crumbling walls.

Scripture reading (Isaiah 46:4):

I will still be the same when you are old and gray, and I will take care of you. I created you. I will carry you and always keep you safe.

Prayer~

Dear Heavenly Father,

Help me to see the beauty in my wrinkles! I have earned them by living this life in my temporary home. Remind me that I may be older, but I still have a lot of work left to do here for your kingdom.

In the name of Jesus Christ, I pray, amen.

This week: ♡ 💪

Each day, spend time remembering your childhood: broken bones and crazy adventures. Write one down every day and smile. Every adventure, every bump along the way, has made you who you are today. Celebrate who you are today! On the final day of the week, make a list of ways you are still able and willing to serve the kingdom.

Are You Okay?

"Hey Lady...Are You OK?"

Photo credit: Shutterstock

New dress—black, to try and make me feel thin. New shoes—red, with stiletto heels to make the outfit pop. I thought I was looking pretty good!

Looking good takes time, so I was running late. I parked my black Subaru (black is apparently a thing for me), stepped out of the car, and put one shoe directly in a melted, gooey pile of what I could only imagine was a full pack of well-chewed watermelon bubble gum.

Instead of taking the pump off, I leaned over, balancing myself on the open car door to try and scrape the gum off my pretty red shoe. The last thing I remember before opening my eyes again was my ankle giving way and grabbing the door.

Did I mention—I was in the Walmart parking lot? In my rush to get where I was going, I made a quick stop by Walmart for, you guessed it—red lipstick to match my gum-covered shoes. My daughters have always teased me that as any true Southern mother, I never leave home without hairspray and lipstick (#Truth).

When I opened my eyes, two wide-eyed teenage boys were peering down at me and asking, "Hey, lady, are you ok?"

Let me think for a minute. I was lying in the Walmart parking lot with my dress now stuck in watermelon gum as well as my amazing red shoe, and my head really hurt. I was not sure where my purse went. There was a young man with what appeared to be a blue Mohawk standing over me. His friend was wearing a Fleetwood Mac T-shirt. What year was this again? I was not wearing lipstick. I was late. Was I, in fact, okay?

It's in moments like these that I know I cannot be alone in questioning my life. Who cares if my lipstick matched the shoes? Why did I feel more comfortable in a black dress than my favorite color, red? Why on earth was I in such a rush all the time? Am I okay? I looked around, and I didn't see anyone else lying in the parking lot. I assumed that meant everyone else had their life together except for me. For a second, I thought I might burst into tears, but then I felt an overwhelming sense of comfort and heard a soft whisper, "You *are* okay."

Life is hard. I am like women everywhere and feel as though I have to be some kind of a perfect life-handling machine. The truth is, I struggle in many of the very same ways every other woman struggles. I try to balance work, family, friends, commitments, and what seems like an ever-growing list of to-do items. I compare myself to others and can be insecure sometimes.

Some days I roll like a rock star and others—I lay in a parking lot covered in gum. You know what? That's OK! The only perfect person to ever walk this earth was Jesus Christ. That means it's okay for me to lose focus, get in a rush, and make a bit of a fool of myself in front of strangers. Tomorrow will be another day. Perfection is off the table.

Maybe God was trying to humble me a bit? I imagined him laughing a little and saying, "Girl, forget about that lipstick! You have important things to do for the kingdom today!" That image brought a smile to my face as I sat up and said to the growing crowd of onlookers, "Yes, I am okay. I will be just fine." Not only did I say the words, but I knew they were true. I *will* be fine and so will all of you! ♡

Scripture reading (Proverbs 3:26):

You can be sure that the LORD will protect you from harm.

Prayer~

Dear Heavenly Father,

Help me laugh at myself a little more this week. Remind me that I don't need to be perfect for the world, because I am *yours*.
In the name of Jesus Christ, I pray, amen.

This week: ♡ 💪

Focus on what you are doing well! Each day, write down three things you did well! They do not have to be huge life-altering things. If by the end of the week you are adding more things to your list, celebrate! God created you for His purpose. Wear His creation with honor. ♡

The Clock

My mother passed away a year ago after a courageous battle with Alzheimer's. Whenever I visit my father now, the ticking of the grandfather clock in the living room they shared seems so much more pronounced to me.

Sitting in the room surrounded by pictures of our family, my eyes are drawn to the snapshots of her smile and my ears to the sound of that ticking clock.

I remember listening to the clock ticking on Thursdays with Mom, waiting for the time to pass from when she thought I was her sister to the silence and blank stares then back to the momentary awareness with eyes straight on me as the words "I love you, Kim" were spoken (the clock ticking).

When I was fifteen, waiting to be sixteen so I could drive, she would say, "Time seems to drag now, but just you wait." She said the same thing when I was seventeen and couldn't wait to be eighteen so I could vote. The words were spoken to me by her over and over again throughout the course of rushing through my life.

So as I sit, watching this man reflecting on the pace his own life has taken, I hear the *ticktock* of this clock. I drift back to my last moments with her—holding her hand, the clock ticking. We all spend so much time rushing to get from one place to another in our lives! Often, once we get there, our focus has already moved on to where we need to be next.

At a recent meeting, I was handed a simple white card with small words in the bottom right corner that read "because I said I would." The idea being to write a promise or commitment that I would keep simply because I said I would.

I wrote "I will be present." In every moment of my crazy hectic life, I will slow down and quiet myself enough to hear the clock ticking.

I often think of Acts 1:7 where we are reminded: "You don't need to know the time of those events that only the Father controls." Not for us to know—we don't know when the next tick of the clock could change everything in this temporary home. Worrying about what will happen next, rushing through days, will only rob you of precious moments: moments of joy, moments of sadness, moments of frustration that turn to moments of real progress, and moments of great love and of great loss.

Can you hear the clock ticking? Don't listen to remind yourself that this life is fleeting. Instead, listen for the opportunity each tick of the clock gives you today, in *this* moment, to be fully present. I am going to "because I said I would."

Scripture reading (Acts 1:7):

Jesus said to them, "You don't need to know the time of those events that only the Father controls."

Prayer~

Dear Heavenly Father,

Help me to be fully present this week. Help me to notice the people around me and to really hear what they are saying to me.

In the name of Jesus Christ, I pray, amen.

This week: ♡ 💪

Take your watch off! I am not kidding. Don't miss work or shut off your alarms, but put your watch away and try not to focus on the clock ticking this week. Be *in* every moment. Each day, write one word about how living without your watch made you feel.

Hannah, the Squirrel

Photo credit: Shutterstock

Outside of my kitchen window stands a row of bird feeders. My husband put them up several years ago after listening to me talk about watching birds with my grandmother. It was a sweet surprise. To be honest, over the years, it has become much more of a squirrel-watching area. He has probably tried every bird-feeding contraption ever made to keep squirrels out, and nothing ever worked. We fed far more squirrels than we did birds—for years.

About a month ago, he proudly announced that he had acquired two guaranteed squirrel-protected bird feeders. As if he had designed and patented them himself, he showed me how the feeders would close with the weight of the squirrel, forcing them to give up in frustration.

For thirty days, I drank my coffee and watched out of my window as squirrel after squirrel attempted and failed to get to the birdseed. They swung and hung and hurled their bodies all sorts of ways trying to get to the food. All gave up except for one—Hannah, the squirrel.

Yes, I named her in honor of her persistence as I watched her attempt to break the code of these feeders—over and over again. Female squirrels work harder than males, so her relentless efforts proved she was in fact: female. Around day twenty-eight, you could see her efforts shift. Hannah became a little quicker to stop fighting the feeder. However, instead of giving up for the day, she would lounge herself on the rail that linked the feeders and just stare.

You think I am crazy, but I am telling you this squirrel stretched out, took in the sun, and looked as if she were studying the feeders for thirty minutes at a time. No further effort, just this same routine for three days. On day thirty-one, I looked out of the window as Hannah methodically made her way from tree branch to shed to rail to the first feeder. She did not attempt to scale the side of the feeder at all. Instead, she simply unscrewed the top of the feeder and plunged inside to a breakfast bowl full of bird feed! Pure genius! 🐿️

I laughed out loud and then clapped for the girl! She was #fearless! She did not let one failed attempt keep her from trying. In fact, she did not let thirty failed attempts keep her from coming back to try again and again. She had true grit!

Let's face it, the other squirrels had to be laughing at her every day. They had given up long ago. We were laughing at her. Heck, even our dog was laughing at her failures for the first few days. Then something shifted, and we began to root for her success. Some days, I think the birds may have even wanted to help her out. They felt so sorry for her. But Hannah did *not* let how she thought any of us felt keep her from the goal.

Each failed attempt made her more determined. She learned something new every single day about what worked and what did not. She learned the rewards of being relentless and fearless are many. She showed the rest of us how to be brave!

She is now a rock star and clearly the designated genius of our backyard animal kingdom. Was she the smartest? Or was she the most determined? Was her prize the birdseed, or the feeling of accomplishment from seeing the mission through to completion?

Life throws so many obstacles at us each day. Fun suckers steal our joy when we brainstorm out-of-the-box ideas with taunts like,

"That will never work!" Negative nellies turn a failed attempt into a sealed coffin of bad ideas instead of an opportunity. The hammer slams down with a judgmental "I told you that would never work."

Hannah knew how to shut the noise out to not become discouraged and to stay focused. We can all learn some things from our squirrel who busted that guarantee into a million pieces.

Be focused. Be determined. Be courageous. Do not let the world discourage you. God is with you.

♡ #BeFearless #BeLikeHannah.

Scripture reading (Joshua 1:9):

I've commanded you to be strong and brave. Don't ever be afraid or discouraged! I am the LORD your God, and I will be there to help you wherever you go.

Prayer~

Dear Heavenly Father,

Help me be brave! I want to be strong and encouraged as I stay focused on your will for my life. Remind me that even when things get tough, if I remain faithful and steadfast in my faith, all things are possible!

In the name of Jesus Christ, I pray, amen.

This week: ♡ 💪

Think about something that is frustrating you this week. Each day, write down one idea to make it better and give it a try! If you fail, try again and again. Be brave. Be strong. Be determined. Celebrate the ways you were all of these things even if it will take more time to move from frustrated to free!

Treading Water

Photo credit: Shutterstock

ife is hard for everyone. Sometimes, we can become so caught up in our own struggles that we lose sight of battles others face. We focus on what someone didn't do one day instead of the hundreds of ways they helped on others. We dwell on how awful our own days have been, never stopping to consider that people are sinking quietly right beside us.

We are human. We are flawed. We are hard on ourselves some days and hard on others the next.

When speaking to groups, I often talk about the power of 10. Basically, it refers to nine things happening that drag our emotions from happy to sad, stressed to excited, thankful to angry, and then the tenth thing happens—and we snap. The tenth thing is usually something trivial and is rarely what actually makes us break. One to nine, the buildup unresolved, is what breaks us. Grace. We all need a little more grace.

There are days we will give more than others. There will be days when others run rings around us. There will be days we are the best friend ever and days when we are so overwhelmed, it is all we can do to like ourselves much less anyone else.

Some days, we will feel like rock stars doing everything right, and still other days, nothing falls into place.

We are all treading water, just trying to stay afloat and breathe. When we think our problems are the worst, all it takes is a moment of reflection to acknowledge the reality that we are all struggling. Different stories, different bodies of water, but we are all treading water.

The only perfect friend is God. Everyone else is human. No matter what body of water you are swimming in today, you are not alone. Swim with *grace*. Tread with *faith*. *Love* with forgiveness.

Scripture reading (Isaiah 43:2):

When you cross the deep rivers, I will be with you, and you won't drown. When you walk through fire, you won't be burned or scorched by the flames.

Prayer~

Dear Heavenly Father,

Help me to live my life with more grace. Forgive me and help me to forgive others so that I can stop treading water and learn to swim in your love.

In the name of Jesus Christ, I pray, amen.

This week: ♡ ✋

Remember a time in your life when it felt like you were treading water. Close your eyes and really pull up all those memories. Who were the people who helped you make it through that difficult time?

Consider writing them a letter or sending a card to let them know how much their grace meant to you.

Take a moment to think about the people who are sharing your life now. Is anyone struggling? Find a way to show grace to them this week.

Kissing Frogs

Photo credit: Shutterstock

Raising daughters, I often told them they would be kissing a lot frogs before they found their princes. Looking back, I must seem like a genius to them at this point!

The thing about frogs is they can be endearing, right? Some are cute. They don't need to drink—so low maintenance. A bunch of frogs together is called an army, which makes them sound cool. Over the years, I may have made frogs sound just cool enough to make them attractive during their rebellious years while at the same time unintentionally making it seem as if my girls needed rescuing by some heir to a throne riding around on a white horse.

The good news is that like all mothers, I learned the fault in my thought process early on! I don't want girls who need to be rescued. I want warriors! By golly, I got them too! They left the frogs croaking in the ponds and realized they already serve a king. Any prince would be a letdown; although, for at least one of mine, the white horse would be nice.

I am thankful to God that they were raised surrounded by strong male role models. They set a high standard for what marrying a "prince" would look like.

Clearly, from the spouses they have committed to walking through life with, they were paying attention. So, ladies, who are looking—there will be frogs along the way. Choose a man who serves your king, and you will never need a prince.

Scripture reading (Song of Songs 8:7):

Love cannot be drowned by oceans or floods; it cannot be bought, no matter what is offered.

Prayer~

Dear Heavenly Father,

Thank you for the gift of love! Having a partner to walk through this life with is such a blessing. Help me be grateful every day for this gift you have given.

In the name of Jesus Christ, I pray, amen.

This week: ♡ ☝

If you're looking for love, double-check this week to make sure you are looking in the right places! Also, make sure your checklist is leading you closer to someone who has the qualities that really matter.

If you're happily not looking, find a way to show gratitude for those qualities that make your spouse a keeper.

Going Home

Photo credit: Shutterstock

My children used to laugh at me because I would do a major house clean before we left for vacation. I wanted to walk in the door and just *be* at home.

Over the early years of their adulthood, they have come to understand. Opening the door to your home after being gone should come with a big restful sigh of relief. They aren't laughing at me anymore. There really isn't anything quite like home. We feel at peace because we know where every scuff mark originated. We feel safe because we know our neighbors. We feel sheltered because we love the people who, over the years, have made our house—a home.

This week, a special young woman died—a wife, a loving mother, a new grandmother, a sister, a daughter, an aunt, a friend. Years ago, when she married, she moved away from her childhood home and planted roots far away. Her roots grew into a beautiful family all her own. Coming home to visit her mother and siblings was difficult due to the distance. Not long ago, she was diagnosed with stage 4 cancer. As her illness quickly progressed, she wanted to come home. Yes, to see her family here—but also to see the ocean and put her toes in the warm water, to smell the meatloaf only her mother could make, to see the face of her sister as they laughed together. To just *be*.

During her visit, she went to her eternal home. Each step in her journey took her one step closer to the home we all seek. Most of us will leave our childhood homes and create our own. Yet, we can all remember what it felt like to enter the door of that home, even as adults, and feel as though we belonged.

Today, I choose to forget the frail and pain-filled earthly body of her last day on earth. I close my eyes, and I see her standing hand in hand with the Father, both with their toes in the warm ocean as the sun rises. I believe she has walked through the door of her eternal home with a sigh of relief and was welcomed by the Father who has created a place just for her, a place where she belongs—a place of peace. She is home.

Scripture reading (John 14:2):

There are many rooms in my Father's house. I wouldn't tell you this unless it was true. I am going there to prepare a place for each of you.

Prayer~

Dear Heavenly Father,

Thank you for preparing a place for each of us! Help us remember your words when we lose loved ones from this—our temporary home.

In the name of Jesus Christ, I pray, amen.

This week: ♡ 💪

Spend some time this week remembering loved ones who have died. Write down some of your favorite things about that person. Do you remember his/her smile or laugh? Take a moment before you close your eyes this week to be thankful for the opportunity God freely gives us and to be with our loved ones forever.♡

The Other Woman

Photo credit: Shutterstock

Thirty-one years of marriage, and the last thing I ever worried about was another woman. Daisy has changed all that. Weighing in right at 90 lbs. with big, brown eyes, this nearly toothless German shepherd has slowly finagled her way into the life of my husband. She sits between us at the dinner table each night. She has a standing "date" with him every Sunday morning as they ride through town together before church.

One week, our pastor who lives in our neighborhood asked me why I had ignored him when he waved. "When?" I asked him. "This morning when you and Larry rode by." I paused for a moment to clarify. "This morning?" He shook his head and looked at my husband for help as I barked back, "I am sorry our dog Daisy did not wave at you." But seriously, the only thing we have in common is brown eyes.

The man shed, meant as his personal place to escape, has become their nightly meeting place to share pork rinds and watch sports together.

Even on nights when we all pretend to share the living room, she makes her place in his life very clear. If I dare sit beside him on the couch to watch TV, she paces and makes strange noises, and if I still don't move, she paws me. As soon as I give in and move to the love seat, she takes her rightful place beside him.

I get sick and my husband kisses me bye as he heads to work. Once when I had a stomach bug, he would toss things at me, trying not to catch whatever was punishing me. Daisy got sick a while back, and he slept on the floor beside her.

Last week, when I called to say I was running late for dinner, he responded, "No worries! I will fix steaks for me and Daisy." I wondered if there would be wine.

Some might say Daisy must treat him better than I do; that is possible. I have teeth, and I talk a lot more. I don't like pork rinds and prefer the air-conditioning inside of our home. I could be jealous. I do think it's a unique and strange, in a good way, relationship. But I am not gonna lie. When I watched him sleeping on the floor beside her and carrying her outside when she was too weak to walk, I realized I had a pretty great husband. I think that capacity for love has room for more than one brown-eyed girl.

Scripture reading (1 Corinthians 16:14):

Show love in everything you do.

Prayer~

Dear Heavenly Father,

Open my heart that I may be open to the love this world offers. Help me to show love in all of my actions and choices this week.

In the name of Jesus Christ, I pray, amen.

This week: ♡ 💪

Think about the pets who have added so much to your life. Find a way to help the animal shelter in your community.♡

Life of a Swing

Photo credit: Shutterstock

The secrets of our family are all held by our front yard glider swing. It was a housewarming gift from my mother over twenty years ago. It has served us well.

She has gently rocked us as I read my girls stories in the afternoon shade of summer. Pillows and blankets have made it home for hundreds of naps.

She has helped us watch thousands of days end. We swing until the sun fades completely behind the trees on the creek bank. The swing has listened to many a dream be shared as we counted stars in the night sky.

The swing has proudly centered herself for Thanksgiving family pictures over the years. She has carefully and gently rocked grandparents as they watched their grandchildren kayak by, with a wave in their direction.

Many a tear has been shed within the safety of her frame—tears of loss when friends died, tears from breakups and makeups, tears during difficult transitions in our lives. She held us through it all and just listened. The swing has been a place of solitude over the years: pretending to read a book in her arms when, really, I was waiting for my girls or my husband to return safely in the boat, pulling in the yard from a late meeting to see my husband waiting in the swing for me with Daisy by his feet.

She held the secrets of teens sneaking out their bedroom windows to rendezvous in the safety of her discreet location—first kisses, last kisses, dreams of kisses, and a million familiar kisses. Oh the tales she could tell! It's strange to think of one inanimate object being able to play such a significant part of our family story. Yet, so many of our moments have come to life on this swing. If she could talk, would she talk of hurricanes and woodpeckers, or would she talk about us?

Our history, our secrets, our love have all been chapters in the life of a swing.

Scripture reading (Psalm 71:9):

Don't throw me aside when I am old; don't desert me when my strength is gone.

Prayer~

Dear Heavenly Father,

Give me the strength to bear the happy and sad times in life for myself and those I love. Help me be a comfortable support for them like a strong glider.

In the name of Jesus Christ, I pray, amen.

This week: ♡ 💪

Look around your home. Is there an inanimate object that holds your family secrets? What is it? Write or draw about it so you can bring it to life for your family.

Unpack Your Baggage

Photo credit: Shutterstock

I magine you are with me as I prepare to leave for work this morning. I have my hairspray, my lipstick, and my navy-blue blazer. I am clutching my iPad Pro which stores much of my life. I have my smartwatch to keep me on schedule. It also beeps should my heart stop, should I need to calm down and breathe, or should I need to stand up because I've been sitting too long (that's probably an issue for another blog). You hold the door open for me, and it appears I am dragging something behind me.

You can't see anything, but you notice my shoulders slumped and my body slowed by the weight of something. You walk around me and see nothing. You ask me if I am OK, and I reply, "Sure!" What you can't see in me and what we can't see in each other is the enormous baggage we all carry—the emotional wounds that never healed and now have become scars. The weight of the wounds we carry with us into every aspect of our lives isn't clearly visible, but we know it's there.

Imagine how large the suitcase would be if every emotional wound from the time we were born was placed on a sticky note and kept in an actual piece of luggage: everything from hurt feelings and broken hearts to jobs we didn't get and huge disasters of our own creation. The luggage would include all the words said in anger, the times trust was eroded, and the wounds from people who walk through life with two faces just to keep us on our toes.

Wounds for many are incredibly deep—abuse, acts of violence, life-altering events that make carrying the baggage alone impossible. Impossible, that is, unless and with help, some of the baggage can be unpacked. Even when we think our baggage is too heavy a load, we need to remember: we are never alone.

In my life, I deal with a lot of people, and a lot of people deal with me. Sometimes, someone reacts to a discussion in a completely unexpected way, and everyone pauses, thinking, *Where did that come from?* Sometimes, I react in a totally unexpected way, and everyone is looking at me wondering, *What has gotten into her?*

Those unexpected eruptions of emotion are from our unpacked baggage. If we have been betrayed, we lose trust. From that point, we may say we trust, but we verify everything whether in our professional or personal lives. People we care about believe they have to prove their loyalty time and time again.

If we've been in a situation when we felt we had no control, we sometimes try to control *every* little and big thing so we never have to feel that loss of control again, *ever*.

We think we have been treated unfairly, and we see that wound open up in interactions all around us. We start trying to fix things that were never broken.

Wounds not carefully treated can become scars that show up for the rest of our lives. They serve as a visual reminder of the injury, taking us back to that moment over and over again for the rest of our lives. We need to unpack so that we can be present and live fully.

A lifetime of wounds is a lot of baggage. I am not a therapist or a spiritual counselor. I am a woman trying to get through life the best way I know how like many of you. So I can't tell you how to unpack your baggage. I can only pray that you do, that we all do.

Life is ahead of us! We need to lighten our load.

Scripture reading (Psalm 147:3)

He renews our hopes and heals our bodies.

Prayer~

Dear Heavenly Father,

I cry out to you to help me lighten my load. The baggage from years of struggle is keeping me from moving forward. Help me to unpack it all and let it go.

In the name of Jesus Christ, I pray, amen.

This week: ♡ ♆

Pull out a small suitcase. Get some sticky notes or index cards. Start writing. Write one thing only on each card. Fill that suitcase with the hurts, lies, and brokenness that you have been carrying around for far too long. Do this every day, and at the end of the week, empty your suitcase and throw it all away. Let it go so that you can become all that God wants you to be in this life.

Pressure Cookers

Photo credit: Shutterstock

Growing up, I worked at an old-fashioned snack bar that was inside Bob Clarke's family-owned pharmacy. Not to give my age away, but we had an entire aisle of penny candy, and we all wore white nurselike uniforms with the required pantyhose. Other than the fact I had to work every day after school and on the weekends, I loved my job! So many nice people came in who would order coffee and share their lives with me. They also did a lot of praying for me because I was not the greatest employee. I was on time. I was dependable. I was also in teen hormone-induced la-la land.

One Sunday morning, the son of the owner and I opened the store. One of my favorite customers was there as soon as the store lights flipped on for his morning coffee.

Wooden swinging doors, like you see in the saloons of old Western movies, separated the snack bar from the storage room. Mr. Clarke had left a note to remind me to prepare the chicken using the pressure cooker in the storage area. I followed the directions exactly—sort of.

Thirty minutes or so later, a really great joke the customer was telling me, as I refilled his coffee cup, was rudely interrupted by a loud boom as the wooden doors burst open.

The owner's son and I ran to the storage area. We both stopped and just stared at the aftermath. I looked in his direction at the exact moment a celery stalk fell from the ceiling and landed on his head. Silence followed. We both looked around the storage room. Boxes stacked three stories high were covered in pieces of chicken, stalks of celery, bits of onions, and carrots. It was hard to find one inch of that large room not touched by chicken parts. I've struggled eating chicken ever since.

By this time, all the regulars had arrived for coffee. Instead, they grabbed mops and rags to help us clean up. They climbed ladders to collect rogue pieces of carrots, all the time mumbling under their breath, "Hurry before he gets here!" Clearly, they thought my hours were numbered. Bob Clarke was a generous and loving man. He is one of the many men who I watched growing up and saw Christ in their actions. He helped so many people with medicines they could not afford. When I was older, I learned how he helped my own parents when my brother was dying. He was a good man, but his storage room was ruined; even good men have their limits.

We scrubbed and we scrubbed. When I came out of the storage room, several of my regular Sunday morning-snack bar crowd had made coffee and had kept the other customers happy.

We never spoke of it again. It was as if they knew the exploding pressure cooker was symbolic of the teenage angst at that point in my life. They just helped me. No judgment. I am sure they laughed about it with the new girl after I went to college. I don't even care because in that moment, they did not let an exploding chicken ruin my life.

Scripture reading (Ecclesiastes 4:10):

If you fall, your friend will help you up. But if you fall without having a friend nearby, you are really in trouble.

Prayer~

Dear Heavenly Father,

Thank you so much for filling my life with people who will help me when I fall.
In the name of Jesus Christ, I pray, amen.

This week: ♡ 💪

Think about a time when you were so glad to have someone there to help you. If possible, tell them thank you. Be that person for someone else this week.

Rethink the Wardrobe

Photo credit: Shutterstock

When I was a child and we talked or sang about the armor of God, images of knights on white horses always came to mind. The bad guys were clearly visible, and the good guys always won. I never really imagined myself suited up, but I sure loved the idea of being protected by the armor built by my faith in God—just for me.

As an adult, the images are not all that different. I still picture actual armor, but I am wearing it myself instead of a random knight. I am still growing into my faith. The bad guys are rarely clearly visible and, on the surface anyway, it seems like the good guys lose quite often. On the surface…

Without sharing the messy details of my life, lately, I feel like parts of it are being attacked from all sides. Actual people are not pulling out weapons but roadblocks that could easily make some throw their hands up and walk away—are coming at me from all directions. Not one, not two, *many*. Did you notice how I made that all about me? It has *nothing* to do with me in reality and everything to do with the work we try to do in the name of God.

I was reminded today by a special pastor that when the work of God begins to make an impact in the world, that is exactly when those serving as His hands and feet need to suit up the most! Attacks will surely follow!

This afternoon, I read Ephesians 6:10–20 and fell asleep (because I stayed up all night worrying) with the Bible in my lap. I dreamed I was standing by a waterfall in full armor with warriors to my left and to my right. They were familiar faces of people I know and love. I was not alone, neither are you.

Let's be encouraged today! If everything is going wrong, maybe the bigger, more important things in life are actually going very right. On days that we can't tell the good guys from the bad, let's keep our eyes on God. When it feels like we are being attacked from all sides, we will help each other remember that we are not alone.

He does not call the equipped—He equips the called!

We've got this! Suit up!

Scripture reading (Ephesians 6:10):

Finally, let the mighty strength of the Lord, make you strong.

Prayer~

Dear Heavenly Father,

Sometimes I do not feel strong enough to do the things I know you are asking of me. Help me feel your presence and know that when I'm afraid, I am not alone.

In the name of Jesus Christ, I pray, amen.

This week: ♡ 💪

Each day, spend time reflecting on a time you were afraid. Think back now that the fear has passed: can you see now how God was with you?

Sunset

Thousands of people flock to Oia (Greece) to watch the sun set each night. They line the streets, the shore, the rooftops. At first, not going to lie, I couldn't figure out the big deal. The sun rises and sets every single day, right? Then I saw it. The massive sunset seemed to fill the sea. It was as if the entire world was saying good night at the same time. "Sunsets are proof that any day can end beautifully" was written on the entrance to one viewing area. How true.

It's hard to imagine not feeling hopeful about what tomorrow will bring when you end a day completely enveloped with such amazing natural beauty. Standing there, all I could think about was how much we take for granted how many sunsets we miss working late or in meetings, how many sunrises we skip checking our emails or at the gym, or how much of life we miss worrying about what will come next.

What would happen if we paused each day at sunset to reflect and be thankful? What if we saw a sunset as much as a beginning as and end? Standing there with thousands of people from all around the world speaking so many different languages and all looking in one direction, was, for me, just as spectacular. Imagine.

Scripture reading (Psalm 113:3)

From the dawn until sunset the name of the Lord deserves to be praised.

Prayer~

Dear Heavenly Father,

Thank you for the beautiful reminder that each ending opens the way for a new beginning!
In the name of Jesus Christ, I pray, amen.

This week: ♡ ✍

Make a point to watch each sunset for a week. Write down something you are grateful for from the day that is ending. Then jot down something you are excited about for the next day! Begin to see the sunset as a beginning, not just an ending.

Tightrope

Photo credit: Shutterstock

I have this dream every now and again. It's always raining. I am usually listening to '80s rock, Journey, most nights. Sometimes I am wearing shoes, and other times, my feet are bare. I am always walking on a tightrope.

As a young mother, the tightrope of life forced me to balance trying to be a supermom with trying to be a devoted wife, while work and other commitments threatened to take me crashing down at any given moment.

When my girls became young adults and headed off to college, the tightrope forced me teeter between holding on to every detail of their lives and letting go so they could live the lives God had in store for them. Balancing this stage made me feel like one wrong move would send me spiraling out of control and take them with me!

Maneuvering the sandwich phase (helping both children and parents), I lost balance every other day—a little every single day if I am being honest. There is no controlling or even anticipating what a day for someone living with Alzheimer's will bring, but balance is not on the list. Was I ever really in control at all though? As a young mother, I put ridiculous expectations on myself. I read every parenting book and article ever written. I filled the house with great literature, listened to classical music while they were still in the womb, violin lessons, dance lessons—you name it. Yet none of that prepared me for the day two of their neighborhood friends were killed.

"Wait a minute, God! How am I supposed to explain to them that in this world, full of beauty and opportunity, children can be killed while playing in the front yard?" My tightrope shook; I lost my balance. "What would happen if" took hold of my legs. In the midst of trying to hold on when they headed off to college, my tightrope was pretty steady. They were both doing well, putting themselves through on scholarships for the most part. The world was getting smaller as they began traveling and studying abroad. Things were good; I felt balanced.

Early one morning, the phone rang, and I could not understand one word being said through the sobs. One of their friends had taken his own life. My tightrope shook; I lost my balance. "What will happen if" started tugging at me.

"Wait a minute, God! In a world so beautiful, just waiting to be experienced, how can this happen to someone so amazing?"

Even when you love every minute spent with a mother who is slipping away, you lose balance and certainly all control. "Wait a minute, God! How can a woman so together all the time become this confused, lost soul who is in front of me?"

The thing about walking a tightrope is that we are usually balancing our lives on the wrong things—myself included. We try to balance between what the world expects *of* us and what we expect *from* it instead of what God wants *for* us. We miss Him saying to us, "Wait a minute!" We spend so much time driving children from one thing to another when they are young, we often don't slow down enough to enjoy lazy snuggles. We schedule everything on perfectly organized color coded (yes, I color coded) calendars, and when one thing goes wrong, we slip off that tightrope.

As the children get older, we start trying to prepare them for life with all the right courses and all the right opportunities, adding pressure to get them ready for what the world defines as success. We push and plan so much so we often miss the part of life that will save them when their tightropes shake—the things they *love*. All of the wonderful, creative, soul-quenching things they love can get pushed aside as we prepare them for adulthood. The very things that will help them fulfill their purpose can so easily get lost in the shuffle.

When our parents need us, we question the fairness of life. We try to make their care fit into our scheduled lives. We teeter all over that tightrope ready to go over at any minute. We forget that each moment is an opportunity for a memory that many people just wish they could have again. We lose our faith: faith in God, faith in each other, faith in our family, faith in friends, faith in love, faith in our ability to balance our lives even when strong winds come—and we all know they *will* come—and faith in what each tomorrow *can* bring for our lives and those we love.

I am learning (not there yet) that the more I let go of trying to control every aspect of my life, the fewer tightrope dreams creep in on me. In every situation, I try to keep my balance by looking for what I can learn from the experience instead of asking God why or how he could let it happen in the first place. I am learning to pull myself out of the belly of the whale and look for ways to grow.

Today, I try to be present for whatever happens and for each person who crosses my path. I am much more focused on each moment instead of planning them weeks and months ahead. Worrying about everything that may or may not happen tomorrow will just add to my wrinkles. Baby steps! I am still trying to control some things!

Scripture reading (Matthew 6:34)

Don't worry about tomorrow. It will take care of itself. You have enough to worry about today.

Prayer~

Dear Heavenly Father,

Thank you for worrying enough for both of us! You've got this, and I am grateful! Help me focus today on *today*, letting the cares of tomorrow wait.

In the name of Jesus Christ, I pray, amen.

This week: ♡ ☙

Every morning, write your worries down and place them in your Bible after you have read the Scripture. Give them to God.

Time to Fly

Standing at the bottom of the stairs, I heard her say, "Look, Mommy! I can fly like Peter Pan!" I froze. I had her eight-month-old sister in my arms as she was perched on the loft railing ready to "fly." I could not breathe. The house went up for sale the next week.

Fast forward to high school—she wanted to fly again. This time to see the world! France, Italy, and England were only a plane ride away for her. She stood at the airport security gate, ready to fly. I could not breathe.

Off to college she went. We unpacked her car and squished everything in her dorm room. She was ready to "fly" wherever life took her, and I, once again, could not breathe as we drove away. "But I love him, Mom" turned into a packed up car and a drive toward the man she would spend her life with. At that moment, I struggled for breath. It was admittedly easier though because I knew she wouldn't be flying alone.

Even when she called me to watch her hang from silks at what looked like hundreds of feet above the ground, she appeared to be flying, and I could not breathe. It's a pattern for me obviously. This week, she is packing up to move with that man she loves. As it should be, right? A new dream job in the place she has always wanted to live. Everything she loves all around her, except for me—doggone it! She is ready to fly, and I can't breathe.

Honestly, though part of the reason I can't breathe is that I can't stop crying long enough to catch a full breath. The weird or maybe not so weird thing is that I am not crying from fear or apprehension. Rather, it is absolute joy for seeing her life become her own. She is definitely a #BeLikeHannah kind of woman: determined, smart, hardworking. Yet, when I close my eyes, I still see her two-year-old self with a pink pillow case wrapped around her waist, ready to fly like Peter Pan.

Breathe.

Scripture reading (Proverbs 23:6):

Teach your children right from wrong, and when they are grown they will still do right.

Prayer~

Dear Heavenly Father,

Thank you for blessing my life with warriors for daughters. Help me to relax and breathe knowing that you are in control.

In the name of Jesus Christ, I pray, amen.

This week: ♡ ✍

Make contact with someone who has moved far away in actual distance but who is never far from your heart.♡

Weary Warriors

Sarah Carmody Photography

Each night, when I have finished burning my Yankee Candle, I place the lid on top of the jar and wait. The full flame begins to struggle but eventually gives way to darkness. Watching it some nights, I kind of feel sorry for the flame! It's burning so beautifully, and then I come along to snuff the life out of it.

In many ways, we do that to each other as we make our way through life. Some people have flames burning so brightly, while others worry they will burn themselves out from the amount of effort they give to everyone and everything.

From my own observations, rarely do we burn ourselves out from working too hard or giving too much. Instead, lots of external forces: negativity, cruelty, apathy, and sometimes hopelessness—because no amount of effort can fix some things—smother the flames burning in our hearts until we just become weary.

That quote, "No good deed goes unpunished" comes to mind as I see well-meaning people snuff the flames of others who are doing great things! If you have served on any committee, you know that an energetic person with a lot of passion can often be completely shut down. Passion moves to weariness.

Weary is different than tired to me. When tired, we can still lie down and sleep for eight hours. When we are weary, sleep does not come easily. When we are weary, we are both physically and emotionally exhausted.

Weary people are like the flame in that Yankee Candle jar struggling to keep burning. Weary people have given so much of themselves to everyone else, not much is left to renew their own hearts and souls at the end of the day.

For me, if I am looking for a person who I know will make this world a better place, I look for the weary. I know that weary warriors always find the strength to strap on the armor and get up again. Weariness shows in the eyes of warriors because for them, the work is never done. At the very core of warriors, they feel called to action.

Every tear shed means they care deeply. Every frustration means they want to make things better. Every flame, even if it is just barely smoldering, means the fire is still there to fight another day!

We all get weary at times. We have all had a day when we held it together for ten people and then went around the corner to fall to pieces ourselves. That's OK because when we are weary, we are most able and often more willing to open our hearts to the rest God offers.

Scripture reading (Matthew 11:28):

If you are tired from carrying heavy burdens, come to me and I will give you rest.

Prayer~

Dear Heavenly Father,

Forgive me when I get weary. I forget to come to you and instead try to do everything myself. I burn my candle at both ends and leave no time for you. Thank you for giving me rest.

In the name of Jesus Christ, I pray, amen.

This week: ♡ ☝

Pull out your calendar and schedule time for God every single day. We put everything and everyone else on our planner, and we make it happen. Be intentional. Designate a time for God, and make it happen.♡

Wanting and Walking

Photo credit: Shutterstock

Who can forget Veruca Salt telling her dad she wanted the golden egg in the movie *Willy Wonka & the Chocolate Factory*? When I watched the movie as a child, I was scared for the poor girl dropped down the rotten egg chute. As an adult watching the spoiled child sing "I Want It Now!" I would really like to toss her down the chute myself.

I wonder if that is how God feels when we pray sometimes. He hears so many polite versions of "Dear, God, I want…." Young adults praying to find their soul mates: "Now, please." Young couples praying for children: "Now, please." We pray for the perfect job: "Now, please."

Does He laugh and think we are cute begging him to change the plan? Or does He get irritated and nickname us Veruca as He jokingly ponders the rotten egg chute? I hope He is a patient parent. Prayer is a tricky thing! My mother said, "Never pray for patience! Pray for patience, and God may send ways for you to practice that skill."

Others have said, "Pray for help, and He may send it in ways you never imagined and that are hard for you to embrace."

When I pray, I feel like God is shaking His head and chuckling—not to mock me but to lovingly wait for the day when His child gets it. I don't know all the rules. I just begin.

I am learning to have a conversation. I speak, and then I listen. He already knows everything I need and what I want, so I have started just praying for the good sense to recognize his direction in my life. I admit to sometimes hearing, "Girl, what were you thinking?"

We all pray for assurance before we start walking in a new direction toward what we think we want in life. We need to know it's all going to be OK. Sometimes, I think the not being OK part of life can be the most important part.

God understands we are all at different places in our faith journey. So just pray, guys. Start somewhere, and the conversation will grow. For Christians, I think prayer is the most powerful thing we can do for others and ourselves. It's not the only thing, but it is a great place to begin and end everything.

Remember those thank you notes your mother made you write? Don't forget to give God his too! I feel like gratitude and praise need to happen in any good relationship.

Wanting things in our lives and walking in new directions can be both terrifying and really great things! Just remember to take Him with you on that walk! Walk and talk a little, then walk and listen, then talk some more. Start the conversation.

He wants great things for us too. He also wants a relationship with His creation. It's hard to have a relationship if you never communicate with each other.

Talk, listen, walk this path together. Just begin.

Scripture reading (James 5:13):

If you are having trouble, you should pray. If you are feeling good, you should sing praises.

Prayer~

Dear Heavenly Father,

Thank you for hearing my prayers! You know my soul, and you love me. Even when I pray without stopping to listen, you patiently wait to join the conversation. I am so thankful to be walking through this life—with you.

In the name of Jesus Christ, I pray, amen.

This week: ♡ ✍

Take time to walk and talk, literally. Prayer is a conversation. Go for a walk each day, and as you walk, talk. You talk one way. Then listen on the return trip home. Just listen.

Bag of Friends

Photo credit: Shutterstock

I was sixteen. The blonde-haired, blue-eyed surfer boy of my dreams dumped me. Not in a note that I could read in the privacy of my own home. Instead, he showed up with another girl on a crowded beach—a beach where pretty much my entire high school hung out in the summer. It could have been a humiliating experience if not for someone having my back.

Before the entire dramatic event could unfold, a family friend who was quite handsome in his own right came to my side. He was older and out of high school (so he appeared to be a mysterious older man). Handsome *man* whisked me away in his jeep while surfer *boy* (with no car by the way, just a bike) sat with his mouth hanging open.

My rescuer didn't drive me far, but only he and I knew that. We ended up right around the corner in a Short Stop parking lot. I ugly cried in private for an hour using his beach towel as a tissue. He bought me a root beer while I washed my face in the bathroom, and he never told a soul. Now I tell all of you, warriors!

Friends are a gift from God. They tell you when you have lipstick on your teeth. They won't let you buy clothes that look terrible. They are always truthful with love.

The best thing about friends is they really know you, right? They know if you are nervous about an interview, chocolate chip pancakes will calm the nerves. They give the same words of encouragement your mother gives, but it feels better because the whole obligation of having given birth to you thing is not there.

Friends can call you from where they are hiding inside a closet at a party because they know you will say exactly the right thing to make them walk out with head high and shoulders back, knowing they are enough.

Friends want the best for you, and you want the best for them. They listen to you whine incessantly and then say, "I hear you." They laugh at your stupid jokes or wear all black to sneak in your yard and decorate your car, letting the world know you are officially old. They know your limits.

When you look at the friends Christ kept close, they were quite a mixed bag, huh? Look at your bag of friends. Are they all the same, or do their differences bring great strength to the relationships? Do they bring great strength to you?

This summer, while the weather and the topics are both kind of hot, take some time to be with your friends. Laugh about the crazy stuff. Reminisce about those life-altering moments. Maybe even cry about those, bring you to your knees, memories that make us who we are when all is said and done.

Then take a moment to thank the good Lord for the people he has placed in your bag. Never forget that the best friend you will ever have is our heavenly Father. He created you! So He already loved you before your mama brought you into this world. Keep him in your mixed bag!♡

Scripture reading (Proverbs 27:9):

The sweet smell of incense can make you feel good, but true friendship is better still.

Prayer~

Dear Heavenly Father,

Thank you for the friends you have placed in my bag! Help me to nurture those relationships just as I work on my relationship with you, Father. Thank you for being my most faithful friend of all.

In the name of Jesus Christ, I pray, amen.

This week: ♡ 💪

Make contact with friends near and far! Let them know you are glad they are in your bag!

Bone-Tired

Photo credit: Shutterstock

Staring at my leg covered in ice (shin splints) while simultaneously experiencing the pain in my back from the same thing that gave me shin splints, the word *exhausted* just isn't cutting it. This feels more than tired, more than drained, more than old!

Pain alone doesn't make me feel like this, neither does physical work. This kind of tired comes when your body, your mind, and your heart have all been pushed beyond their normal limits.

For the first time, in a long time, I understand *bone-tired*. My brain is too full. My heart is drained. My body aches. My bones are struggling to keep me upright.

I could try caffeine, but then I would just be vibrating along with everything else. My soul and my body need rest. Yet, looking at the calendar, rest is not coming soon.

So I will wind myself up, paint on a smiling face, and do everything I need to do tomorrow and the next until rest comes. I will go through the motions. I will take Motrin for the pain and cover my legs in Tiger Balm. I will tell everyone I am fine when I am so tired, I can't think. I will secretly want to slap every person who asks me to do one more thing or handle one more problem.

The thing is, I know so many of you reading this are right there with me! Why do we always put ourselves last? That only helps others in the short term. If we want to really give our best, we need to be our best—not a windup doll version. We all underestimate the value of making time to just stop and unplug from the world. I stink at it, guys! Something tells me God may be teaching me.

Scripture reading (Jeremiah 31:25–26)

Those who feel tired and worn out will find new life and energy, and when they sleep, they will wake up refreshed.

Prayer~

Dear Heavenly Father,

I come to you bone-tired, seeking to be refreshed!
In the name of Jesus Christ, I pray, amen.

This week: ♡ 💪

Start with fifteen minutes on the first day, and completely unplug from the world. Turn off the TV, the phone, the iPad—everything. Just be still. Add five minutes each day.

Death of a Snowman

Photo credit: Shutterstock

Where our little creek meets the river is a lovely strip of shoreline only accessible by boat. We meet friends there some days to grill and spend the afternoon. One evening in late summer, I had a brilliant idea. We could take the metal snowman decoration from Christmas last year, stick him in the sand, and take a picture! It would make a great Christmas card! Perfect!

On the boat ride over, I took all kinds of silly pictures with the snowman: driving the boat, fishing off the side, tanning on the front deck. This was going to be an epic Christmas card! When we pulled the boat up on shore, I jumped off and started posing the little guy in the sand. One way, the glare was too bright; another way, you couldn't see enough water. The solution? He needed to be closer to the river.

Just as I went to stick that metal sucker in the sand, I lost my footing. I swear the metal man laughed at me! When I tried to regain my balance, my foot came down on the rotting trunk of what was left of a tree. Pieces of the tree came through my foot in several places, breaking four toes. The blood started flowing from my foot, and everything started spinning. Each time I glanced over, that snowman looked like his smile had become more grimacing. He was mocking me.

Before my ridiculously makeshift-bandaged foot and I got back on the boat to go to the ER, I found a special way to kill the snowman. No Christmas card should ever have that evil smile as a greeting. We strapped him to a tree so that each and every time we visited this island, I could see him—all alone. It may seem a little cruel since it was all my idea, but consider the fact I had to wear Ugg boots all that winter, and I am too old to wear Ugg.

Did I mention that my toes now permanently give the Vulcan sign? People look at my toes, chuckle, and say, "Live long and prosper." His slow death on a deserted island brings me a small measure of vindication. Don't worry, he had a lot of fun before ultimately someone cut him loose. He became quite famous in our neck of the woods! Pictures of visitors with this beached snowman popped up every summer. He had a good life—just not with me!

I sometimes say God "winks" at me. Something happens, and it feels sent from God as encouragement. That day, he humbled my rear end! No wink, just a swift butt kick. The snowman and the big guy upstairs chuckled a bit that day. I deserved it. My toes will never let me forget. "Live long and prosper!"

Scripture reading (Ecclesiastes 2:11):

Then I thought about everything I had done, including the hard work, and it was simply chasing the wind. Nothing on earth is worth the trouble.

Prayer~

Dear Heavenly Father,

Help me to spend my time on things that matter. Help me to not get lost in the superficial and vain trappings of this world.

In the name of Jesus Christ, I pray, amen.

This week: ♡ ✍

Think about times in your life when trying to look good for others took precedence over doing good for God.

Finding Your Voice

E very year, students at a local high school find their *voice*. As part of a poetry unit, they watch a documentary entitled *Louder Than a Bomb* and then compete in a poetry slam competition. Beauty comes from pain, they say. Each year, we listen and watch as the most painful details of some of their lives transform into life-changing moments for everyone in the room. A painful loss brings tears and then love. Body image issues, effects of bullying, the pain of divorce, or struggles with so many issues are shared and then healed. They find their *voice*.

We all have voices. We don't all use them. Sometimes, we are silent because we don't want to risk anger from a friend or colleague. Other times, we are silent because we think others could never possibly understand how we feel. We fear isolation and loss of relationship with others.

These teens conquer both the written and spoken word during this unit of instruction. They learn to speak honestly with confidence. They learn to trust each other. They learn to use their voice and have mastered the art of really listening to another person.

Imagine an experience in your life that shook you to your core. Now imagine sharing that experience all alone on a stage in a darkened auditorium. Imagine the bright spotlight surrounding you as fear begins to take hold. Imagine your friends and colleagues sitting in the audience. The light blinds you, but you know they are there. Will they hear your story and accept you? Will they understand you better and be kinder in the future? Or will you be mocked on social media that night?

Finding your voice takes tremendous courage. Every year, the students cry, laugh, and cry some more. They cheer on students who get choked up at the reality of what they are sharing. Students surround their bravery with love, trust, and acceptance. Finding your voice doesn't mean yelling until people listen. It means finding the confidence to speak your truth in a way that draws people to really listen—they can't turn away. Sharing your voice requires faith that even if people disagree, they will listen for understanding.

With one lesson that could have been a traditional poetry lesson, lives are transformed year after year. Brave teachers who create a safe environment for their students teach both poetry and humanity. Imagine a world this safe, allowing us all to just *be* ourselves. Imagine a world where our voices, all of our voices, are heard and acknowledged by such open hearts. These students show us it's both possible and beautiful.

Scripture reading (1 Peter 3:8–9)

Finally, all of you should agree and have concern and love for each other. You should also be kind and humble. Don't be hateful and insult people just because they are hateful and insult you. Instead, treat everyone with kindness. You are God's chosen ones, and he will bless you. The Scriptures say.

Prayer~

Dear Heavenly Father,

Help me to be compassionate toward people who are hurting. Help me be accepting without judgment or ridicule. Thank you for creating us all equally loved.

In the name of Jesus Christ, I pray, amen.

This week: ♡ ✍

Read and learn more about *Louder Than a Bomb* annual poetry slam in Chicago. Watch a few of the winners share their hearts on stage. Could you? This week, think about the most painful experience in your life. Try setting it to poetry as a beautiful way to release it.

Follow the Leader

Photo credit: Shutterstock

While we were on vacation, I witnessed many tour guides leading groups around city streets. Most often, they had a big sign or card they held up so the crowd wouldn't lose sight of the leader. Herding sheep came to mind as I watched the groups trying to stay together and follow the leader. What if the leader took them in the wrong direction?

One afternoon, as I was sitting in the reading deck of this amazing little bookstore, I watched a guide lead the group straight past where I was sitting. I could see people within the group showing great interest in this home to an entire wall of first edition books with a reading nook overlooking the Aegean Sea, but she hurried them straight past. They also went straight past an amazing museum filled with handcrafted musical instruments from the Byzantine era. All handcrafted and donated by one man for this village he loved.

The fear of being separated from the group kept them from exploring two of the best parts of this little place. They had their eyes on the sign, they were following the leader, and they were missing so much. They felt safe in a group. I wanted them to be brave and explore on their own and develop their own leadership skills!

Being a good leader requires having the heart of a servant. A servant leader would have noticed the interest and stopped. A true servant leader would have known the village inside and out. A servant leader would have spent a little time getting to know the group so they would have a great once in a lifetime experience.

Being that kind of a leader takes a lot of work. It requires the leader to care more about the experience of those they serve than the effort it places on themselves.

In my own life, I have always been slow to follow anyone. I have always marched to my own drum. There have been leaders who inspired me and made me want to work hard for them. Each was a servant leader. Servant leaders never ask someone to do anything they wouldn't do themselves. These types of leaders are just as comfortable leading a meeting as they are sweeping the floor after everyone leaves. They own their mistakes. They encourage. These leaders follow their hearts, their faith, and their principles even when doing so comes at a great personal cost. I would follow a leader like that any day! These type of leaders are hard to find sometimes because they are busy lifting and celebrating everyone but themselves. They are so worth the extra effort to find!

As children, playing follow the leader was a game. As teens, following the wrong leaders could change the trajectory of our lives. As young adults, following the leader could define us in the workplace—for good or for bad. As experienced adults, we have the scars of poor leadership as well as the hearts strengthened by great leadership. We have learned playing follow the leader is anything but a game.

Be careful who you follow in all aspects of your life. The only perfect man no longer walks these streets, so with a true sense of equity, all leaders are flawed. The realization of imperfection makes life become a bit like that childhood game of knowing when it's important to follow the leader and when it might be better to get out of the game.

You can always start your own game and lead instead of follow. *Become* the kind of leader you are looking for in your neighborhood, your church, your place of employment, your life. Just keep your eyes focused on God instead of a group sign, and you will never lose your way.

Scripture reading (Matthew 20:26):

But don't act like them. If you want to be great, you must be the servant of all others.

Prayer~

Dear Heavenly Father,

Help me to stay focused on *you*. Give me strength so that in the absence of good leadership, I can learn to lead as you would have me do.

In the name of Jesus Christ, I pray, amen.

This week: ♡ 💪

Consider the areas of your life where you follow. Are you following good leadership? Is there a way for you to grow in a way that leads others to Christ at your job, your church, in your PTO, or in your neighborhood? What qualities make a good leader to you? Do you have those gifts?♡

Childhood

Photo credit: Shutterstock

My five-year-old bare feet were standing on top of his shiny black shoes. We danced beside a freestanding turntable console that must have been five feet long from Sears, Roebuck and Co. "Moon River" rang through the house as my uncle imagined he was Frank Sinatra, and I imagined nothing but happiness forever.

It's funny. My childhood is filled with family vacations and Little League games. Dance lessons, piano lessons, garage girl bands, and yet the feeling of dancing to Frank Sinatra with someone who was equally as happy to be dancing with me always rises to the top of my favorite memories.

My feet were dirty from playing in the yard while my grandmother cooked dinner. His shoes were shiny because he had just walked in from work. My parents were late picking me up, but that day, I didn't care.

We danced sort of moving like Frankenstein as he lifted each of his legs with mine tagging along for the ride. He sang as if he was Frank, and every once in a while, he would twirl me around, and we'd just laugh.

As a young mother raising my girls, I often thought of this memory. It's tempting to rush our kids through childhood. So many parents feel we need to give our children every possible experience in their young lives. So we go and we go and we go. Do we really? My girls would each give you different answers for their favorite memories from childhood. My favorite two memories of raising them are all about slowing down, not rushing.

The first was an afternoon picnic under a shade tree listening to the public radio summer children's series. We played on a big blanket watching clouds overhead and listened to classical music. The other, an afternoon spent riding two-seater bicycles around Assateague Island. We were there to see the real-life home of Misty from the book series written by Marguerite Henry. It was a simple and slow-paced time together.

This summer, slow down and enjoy the simple moments. Try not to overschedule anyone including yourself. Take time to rest and maybe dance to "Moon River." Take time to just be and to be together.

Scripture reading (Psalm 90:12)

Teach us to use wisely all the time we have.

Prayer~

Dear Heavenly Father,

Help me spend my time in ways that bring honor and glory to you. Time is fleeting, so I want to make the best of it! Let me not be distracted by things that will take my focus from you.

In the name of Jesus Christ, I pray, amen.

This week: ♡ 💪

At the end of each day this week, write down the things from the day that filled your soul and made you smile. Try to adjust your time the next day for more of those things!

Direction

There are days I feel lost and confused, not knowing which way to go or whether I just want to stand still frozen in place. Other days, I feel completely confident in my choices. If we did a remake of *Top Gun*, I would be Maverick-kind of confident. Most days, I am somewhere in the middle of both extremes.

I go to nature when I am feeling lost. For whatever reason, I feel the presence of God more profoundly when I am near the water. So putting the kayak in the water puts me right in the middle of where I need to be when I am feeling lost. I get on the water and just go, waiting for divine intervention to make everything clear for me.

God has this funny way of making me work for His direction. Just like sitting at the end of one branch of the creek wondering which way to paddle, the choice of direction is mine. Sometimes, I choose a smooth route with little resistance and have a peaceful afternoon. Other days, I choose the more difficult path because I know that is the direction I need to take in order to grow and learn.

What I do know is that most days, I end up right where God wants to be in that moment, and I try to follow where he leads me. What does He want me to see or hear right now? What does He want me to learn from this experience? How can I make sure that while I travel the path He sets, people see Him in me?

Having direction in life takes both confidence and humility— kind of like balancing the kayak so you stay on the water instead of in it.

Scripture reading (Proverbs 3:5):

With all your heart you must trust the Lord and not your own judgment.

Prayer~

Dear Heavenly Father,

Help me to be still and quiet long enough to hear and accept your direction for my life. Then give me the courage and strength to follow!

In the name of Jesus Christ, I pray, amen.

This week: ♡ 💪

Where do you feel most grounded? Sketch it or find a photo to place here with this devotion. Write a few words that describe how you feel when you are there. Make a plan to get there soon!

Freckles

(Photo credit: Chad Winstead)

I love freckles. I think of each unique dot as a story from a life well-lived. There is a photograph from the wedding of my youngest daughter that really emphasizes the freckles on her face. Let's forget that she was having makeup applied to try and cover every single one when the photo was taken. I love the photograph! I don't see flaws that need to be covered. I see her life.

I see the days spent riding horses in the hot sun. I hear the trombone playing from her days on the field at band camp. I remember the summer she learned to surf, and if I focus, I can still hear parents screaming in the stands at soccer games.

My mind drifts to her girlfriends' cruises every summer and her zip-lining in Costa Rica when she studied abroad. I remember the photograph of her in the scorching sun in Barcelona and Paris as she helped chaperone high schoolers on the trip of a lifetime.

I see the freckles that popped out when she walked the beaches of Miami. She took in a sunset and realized the hand she was holding was the one she wanted to hold for life. To a mother, freckles on the face of her child are like stars in the sky—each one beautifully and wonderfully made! Each one is a memory, a story, and never a flaw. Why hide such a beautiful life story?

Scripture reading (Psalm 139:13–14):

You are the one who put me together inside my mother's body, and I praise you because of the wonderful way you created me. Everything you do is marvelous! Of this I have no doubt.

Prayer~

Dear Heavenly Father,

Thank you for creating me just as I am! Help me to appreciate your handiwork and to be grateful.

In the name of Jesus Christ, I pray, amen.

This week: ♡ 💪

Stop comparing yourself to everyone else! Seriously. If our daughters see that insecurity in us, they begin to look at themselves differently. So this week, every single day, take five minutes to look in the mirror. Each day, write one thing you like and appreciate about your physical appearance. Beside it, write one thing you like and appreciate about your warrior heart.♡

Fireflies

Photo credit: Shutterstock

There is something so peaceful about watching the sun go down each day. Our work is done. We can rest beneath the shade trees as the light trickles through the leaves. We can be renewed as the breeze becomes a little bit cooler. We can smell the honeysuckle on the vine, and just as the darkness begins to overtake the light of day, we can begin to spot fireflies.

Just one at first, off in the distance of the trees. As the moments pass, more begin to light up until the night is full of tiny specks of light in an otherwise dark place. They are announcing to the world that the warmth of summer is coming!

Did you know that the light of a firefly is the most efficient light on earth? Some light up to attract mates. Others light up to protect against predators. No matter the science of the firefly, they remind us how beautiful even a tiny light can be in the midst of great darkness.

It is easy to become overwhelmed by the absence of light in this world sometimes. The news is full of horrible things happening all around us. We all want a better world for ourselves and for our children. Some days, it can appear like we will be leaving them a cold, dark place. But do we have to accept that as destiny?

We forget sometimes that we are called to be the hands and feet of Christ here on earth. He is always here for us. We need to be here for Him as well. Have we done our part, in our own way, in our own communities, to make this world better? Or have we been more content to let our lights shine from the safety and comfort of our glass jars?

When it gets dark, we need to watch for the tiny lights fighting through the empty shadows. Like fireflies in summer, they are there, waiting to usher in the warmth. We need to join them. Think how efficient and effective the light of a firefly can be, not to mention the joy that the small flash of light can bring. If the light is captured in a jar, it will never fulfill its purpose. Set it free, and imagine where the light will lead others!

We can each be small but powerful lights in the darkness of our own neighborhoods. We can choose to let what people see from us be kindness. We can choose to share love in small ways that grow. We can choose to burn our lights a little hotter at times when the core and the message is grounded in love.

It's not enough to have love and not share it. It's not enough to have the light of Christ in us and not let it burn brightly.

Today, you might be one of the few little lights in a very dark patch of woods. That's OK. In time, the lights will multiply. Have faith in God. Have faith in each other. Believe that millions of little lights can usher in a new season on this earth just as fireflies usher in the warmth of a new summer.

Scripture reading (John 1:5):

The light keeps shining in the dark, and darkness has never put it out.

Prayer~

Dear Heavenly Father,

Some days, this world seems really dark. Help me to find a way to light my small piece of your creation. Let your love illuminate the space around me through my actions this week.

In the name of Jesus Christ, I pray, amen.

This week: ♡ ✍

Write about some of the darkness within your community. Fill the space around it with ideas as you brainstorm ways you can bring light into those dark spaces.

Celebrate!

Photo credit: Shutterstock

Our country has ripped a lot of Band-Aids off lately, exposing wounds that have always been there—they were just covered. Now, all those wounds are in the open air to either infect and slowly kill us or heal and make us stronger.

Life is too short and too valuable for us to choose any option other than heal and make stronger, right? So how do we keep from getting sucked into the negativity and shouting matches?

We celebrate! I am not crazy (well, possibly). Whether negativity and hatefulness happen within our friend base, our workplaces, our churches, neighborhoods, or our families, the people around us are not simply disposable. We can learn something from everyone who crosses our path.

Celebrate the good stuff more! For every negative, find at least two great things that make you smile. Someone ticks you off? Think of two loving things that person has done in the past. If you can't find goodness in someone, the hurt being too deep, forgive them and cut them loose from a place of love. Bitterness and anger will hurt your heart, not theirs.

Our world is full of imperfect people. Those of us who recognize we are not and never will be perfect should be able to forgive slipups in the people around us. We should recognize our own need for grace on an ongoing basis.

If your social media feed is full of stories that are sucking the joy from your soul, unfollow some and intentionally choose a few more joyful things to fill your newsfeed and your heart. I added a happy puppy page to mine so as I scroll and my watch starts beeping for me to breathe, happy puppies playing appear—and I smile.

The evening news making you a little depressed (OK, a *lot* depressed)? Turn it off after you have been informed and then go for a walk. Think about the things in this world that are hurting your heart. Find a way to make those things better in your little corner. Don't stray from the best parts of yourself. Get lost and increase the risk of infection.

Behavior that requires intentionality at first can get as simple as breathing in the love of God and exhaling the feelings generated by the many soul suckers in your life. Celebrating this world God has given us can become a way of living versus a second thought. This past week, I challenged myself to meet doom and gloom with optimism, to follow a negative comment with a celebration. I followed hatefulness with love; it was hard at times. I failed miserably a few times, but I intentionally looked for the good living within my personal soul suckers.

You know what happened? It was a great week! No, my attitude didn't change others (*yet*), but it sure changed me. The more I celebrated, the more I was able to be open to recognizing joyfulness right in front of me.

God is all around us! It's up to us whether or not we celebrate a beautiful sunrise or take it for granted. There are kind people all around us! It's up to us whether we celebrate those who got up on their day off and volunteered in their corner of this crazy world.

To heal wounds requires some intentional extra care for a while. The wounds of our world won't heal with antibiotics or new bandages. Our wounds need grace and love. God gives us both freely. Breathe it in and learn to celebrate something or someone, every day.

Scripture reading (Romans 14:19):

We should try to live at peace and help each other have strong faith.

Prayer~

Dear Heavenly Father,

Help me to silence the noise by turning up the volume on the good stuff! Make me more able to see kindness and love in the world around me.

In the name of Jesus Christ, I pray, amen.

This week: ♡ 💪

Begin and end each day with something funny! Find a puppy video or anything that makes you laugh. Be intentional in beginning the day with laughter. End each day by acknowledging an act of compassion.

Grace

Photo credit: Shutterstock

Standing calmly as someone cusses me out is not an acquired skill. It has taken years of learning the meaning of true *grace*. However, on this particular morning, I am tired. I am also late for work. I am not in the mood for cussing or grace. Can you relate?

Interesting tidbit about myself, I cry *not* when I am sad but when I am mad. I really think this is how God is teaching me grace. It is literally impossible for me to shout back without crying. Then I get more angry with myself for crying, and the ugly cry mixed with snorts begins.

In a weird way, it makes me pause. What has the person in front of me been through this morning? What struggles is she facing in her own life? How was this person raised if this is her learned behavior? The tears when I am mad serve as a pause.

The Bible is full of examples in which God gives grace that we did not earn. He loves us no matter what we do or say in moments of weakness. He sent his Son to die for our sins—the ultimate sign of grace.

Even if the only act of kindness I can muster is to not react in anger and pray for her as she cusses me out, that is enough. I am not going to lie, sometimes I need to walk away and calm down before I can even think about finding grace. The good news is, His grace is sufficient for us all.

Scripture reading (Ephesians 2:8–10):

You were saved by faith in God, who treats us much better than we deserve. This is God's gift to you and not anything you have done on your own. It isn't something you have earned, so there is nothing you can brag about. God planned for us to do good things and to live as he had always wanted us to live. That's why he sent Christ to make us what we are.

Prayer~

Dear Heavenly Father,

Help me extend the grace to others that God extends to me. Help others offer the same grace to me when I fail at being kind.
In the name of Jesus Christ, I pray, amen.

This week: ♡ ✍

Think about a time when you did not show grace to someone. Consider his/her life circumstances and pray about how you can approach the relationship with that person, moving forward.

Can You Pass the GlitterBug Test?

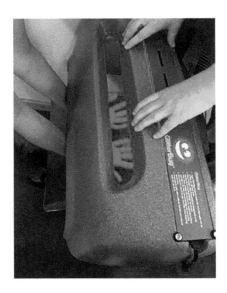

During a recent first aid class for children, the leaders brought out an ultraviolet light called the GlitterBug. Children were taught proper hand washing techniques and then practiced to see how well they listened. After they were done washing, they placed their "clean" hands inside the GlitterBug. Let's just say, it was an enlightening experience for everyone! The children who managed to clean their hands properly received a really cool medal with a picture of this fictional bug. Those who continued seeing germs pop up when their hands were placed under the light kept washing until they were successful.

Standing there watching them, I was imagining a life size GlitterBug for adults. I mean we try and try to wash away our bad behaviors, right? We leave the house in the morning and think we are in good shape. What if we had to walk through a GlitterBug on the way into work? Under the light, would our temper flare up at the stoplight this morning glare back at us? Would the light bring the judgment going through our minds this morning when we looked at our social media feed? What would we look like under the GlitterBug?

The mistake we make as Christians is pretending to the world that perfection in man is even possible. Christians make just as many mistakes as everyone else! We should understand that the only perfect human died for us because He knew we were messy and accepted us anyway. If we really want our faith base to grow and claim hearts for Christ, we have to start owning our imperfections and claiming the struggles we face in our journey toward Christ. People need to know they are not alone. They need to feel worthy. We all do, right?

So next time you glance at someone in a brief moment of judgment, picture yourself inside the ultraviolet light of the GlitterBug. Then smile and give that person a hug from a sincere place of common/shared humanity.

Scripture reading (Matthew 7:1):

Don't condemn others, and God won't condemn you.

Prayer~

Dear Heavenly Father,

Help me to work toward you from a place of acceptance. We are all living with things we need to improve. Open my heart to those seeking to begin the walk toward faith.

In the name of Jesus Christ, I pray, amen.

This week: ♡ ☾

Own the areas in your life that need a little cleaning up. You are not alone!♡

Guard Wanted

(Photo credit: Chad Winstead)

When my first daughter was born, the flaws in my ability to properly use the English language became much more obvious to the general public. Apparently, I used a specific curse word more often than I'd like to admit. This realization came one morning as I was changing her diaper, and she chose to make that word—her *first* word, the word that we will remember forever, the word that goes in the baby book.

She giggled and wiggled and just kept saying it over and over again, for weeks actually. At my mother's house, in the grocery store, at the post office, at church, at the pediatrician's office—she really enjoyed the way it rolled off her tongue and made grown-ups gasp. It was her favorite word. I had used the word with such emotion, so it had to be really special, right?

It's kind of a strange image to think of a guard watching over our mouths, but honestly, our tongues are our most dangerous weapons. Maybe we do need a guard to save us from our word choices. The days of two women sitting on the porch sharing gossip over a bag of Cheetos and a glass of moscato are gone! Those moments have been replaced by people sitting alone in their cars or rooms, making cruel or rude social media posts that spread to millions within thirty seconds. We used to vent to our best friends; now, we vent to the world.

Whether a word spoken in anger or a rumor spread for spite, words have the ability to ruin careers, relationships, and lives. A guard seems reasonable.

Some people say we have all become too sensitive. I disagree. I think we have all become too insensitive. Freedom of speech used to come with a sense of responsibility and respect. We could say what needed to be said without losing our minds—or our dignity.

The ability to communicate with each other in meaningful and honest ways is being lost. We don't talk—we text, we tweet, we email, we Snapchat.

Words are an amazing gift from God! The ability to use them to paint a picture for a reader or to make the music in a song suddenly becomes personal. It can lift people. Words written or spoken in love can take us back twenty years and fill our hearts with joy. Words used in anger or hatred can quite simply, destroy.

I used to be quite a hothead or some might say passionate, both would be accurate. Either choice was equally problematic. Whatever crossed my mind would come flowing out of my mouth, and I would wear the word vomit like a badge of honor. I thought it was somehow admirable to always be completely honest.

With age, a lot of hard lessons learned and a change of heart, I am working on a better balance: truth in love when I need to speak, and sometimes, words are not necessary at all. I have watched too many people lose a good message in their method of delivery. From then on, their words were heard yes, but the message was never received in the same way again, ever.

Anyone can spew hate and then walk away from the fallout. It takes effort to stop when challenged or to vent to the wall if you have to get it out or to breathe and gather your thoughts and only then to look someone in the eye and speak the truth from a place of love. I mess this up regularly; I'm not even going to lie. But I keep trying! #BeLikeHannah

Truth in love is the goal. Yes, even to people who are mean and nasty. I don't enjoy mean and nasty, but my reality might be a guard on one shoulder whispering in my ear, "Respond with truth in love," and the Devil in the other ear screaming, "You aren't going to let them get away with that, are you?"

The balance comes in the end result for me. Do I want a relationship with the person in front of me, or do I just want to be heard? Do I want to make the situation better, or to have my badge of honor stamped across their forehead as I walk away? Or do I, in the pit of my imperfect soul sometimes, want both?

Look around this world right now. Is this really what we want for ourselves, divided up into all-or-nothing groups who shout at, more than we listen to, each other? Does this freedom to spout whatever we want, no matter the cost, make us the model of a free society that should be lifted to emulate? Are we really alright making relationships with people who are not just like us and their ideas so disposable? I will say it makes me feel like I still stand a chance at becoming an OK human being to know that this Scripture is in the Bible! It lets me know that not only do many of us struggle with our words, we've been struggling for a very long time, so we are in this together for the long haul.

Let me repeat that last part because it's *really* important. *We* are in this *together* for the *long haul.* Keep watch, Lord, keep watch over the door of my lips.

Scripture reading (Psalm 141:3):

Help me to guard my words whenever I say something.

Prayer~

Dear Heavenly Father,

Help me to know when to open my mouth and when to keep it closed! Let everything I say be used to improve the situation. May my words always be grounded in your love.

In the name of Jesus Christ, I pray, amen.

This week: ♡ 💪

Be conscious of your words. Each night reflect on times your words helped as well as the times your words may have hurt. ♡

Armor

I wear an armor of one form or another every single day. Each time I am wounded or scarred, I add another layer of protection. What I have found is that sometimes, the act of protecting myself is stifling.

There is a photograph of my oldest daughter wearing actual armor that I love. She is a warrior in life, and the picture is a perfect visualization of how I see her in my mind's eye. She has no fear. Anything she even thinks about trying, she does. She has never let others define her. She walks to the beat of whatever instrument she has in her hand at any given moment in her own beautiful way.

She is fierce in her beliefs and unapologetic if you disagree. Yet, she accepts the differences in others as just that, differences, not walls to relationships.

This millennial put herself through college on scholarship. She took a job way out of her initial comfort zone until she could get the one she loved. She doesn't ask for anything from anyone. Once when a colleague was caught in a nightmare situation, she put her own career at risk to defend him. Without hesitation, she put herself on the line for a person who quite frankly had not always been kind to her because it was the right thing to do.

Armor is for warriors. Even though she wears armor to literally fight, most days, her only protection is the strength of her heart, her faith, and her character. I think she'll be good! I hope I can be as strong of a warrior when I grow up!

Scripture reading (Psalms 28:7):

You are my strong shield, and I trust you completely. You have helped me, and I will celebrate and thank you in song.

Prayer~

Dear Heavenly Father,

Help me be strong and brave for the battles that lie ahead! Battles not just for myself, but battles for friends and family who I love. Remind me, Lord, I wear the armor from my faith in you, 24-7!

In the name of Jesus Christ, I pray, amen.

This week: ♡ 💪

    Each day this week, write the name of someone you know fighting a battle. Pray for them. Find a way to strengthen them. On the final day, acknowledge a battle you are fighting. Pray about the armor you need.

His Eyes

Photo credit: Shutterstock

Today, I saw the eyes of a child that have been burned into my heart forever. A mother and her son came into our church for help. His, maybe, eight-year-old eyes locked with mine, and I could not look away. I tried.

Children come and go every day during the summer feeding program where I volunteer, but this one was different. I tried to get him to play with the other children while his mother sought help. The regulars welcomed him and tried to make him laugh, but he just couldn't. I fixed him a plate of food that he didn't touch. His mother worked with our pastor and volunteers to try and find a solution to their crisis. I watched his mother. My eyes scanned the room where the children were smiling and playing games together. I turned to check on him, and his eyes locked with mine again—there was no joy. There was no sadness either really; there was emptiness. His eyes were blank, and they were glued to mine: no light of hope, no glint of the possibilities life can bring, nothing. Yet, he was somehow speaking volumes to my heart.

So many of the children we serve have parents working multiple jobs. Life is challenging for everyone, and often, their families have hit a rough patch.

We are all one crisis away from needing help. I don't care how many plans you have made, life has a way of sending them all up in flames. For my own family, that is a literal statement. At age five, my family lived in a three-story, with a full basement, beautiful home on the water. For Christmas that year, we received a gorgeous piano. We were living well. A week later, the house burned to the ground, and we were sleeping in a trailer wearing a wardrobe of donations given by our friends and neighbors. My family struggled for years to recover. I repeat for emphasis—we are *all* one crisis away from needing help.

Today, I was tired, exhausted emotionally really. Then Christ showed me why I was where He wanted me to be for His purpose.

By having this child cross my path at quite frankly the exact moment I needed a reminder of what really mattered in life, Christ captured my full attention. People matter, guys. Nothing else really impacts the value and worth of our lives more than the people we know when all is said and done.

His mother got some direction, and they left, but every time I blinked, his eyes were there. I quickly followed them out the door to see if there was any way we hadn't thought of that we could help, but they were gone. It was as if they simply vanished. Yet even now, hours later, his eyes are what I see every time I close my eyes. Where will he be ten years from now? Will he lock eyes with someone along the way who will be able to help him through the long journey of his life? Will his eyes ever light up with joy and hope?

In some ways, I feel as though I looked into the eyes of Christ today. He snapped me right out of my petty issues and focused me in a laser-like way on what and who matters. Children living in poverty are all around us—in *every* community. They need our compassion, our empathy, our help. Christ is making it more difficult for us to simply look away.

Scripture reading (Matthew 25:40):

The king will answer, "Whenever you did it for any of my people, no matter how unimportant they seemed, you did it for me."

Prayer~

Dear Heavenly Father,

Keep my eyes focused on children struggling in poverty. Help me find ways to lift them, and strengthen them for a path that will lead to security in both you and in this world.

In the name of Jesus Christ, I pray, amen.

This week: ♡ 💪

Do a little research. Find out the poverty rates for your community. Explore opportunities to serve children who struggle with food insecurity. Find a way to help.♡

Keep Swimming

Photo credit: Shutterstock

I can't even count the times I have said to people, "Just keep swimming." Bad day? Keep swimming. Work not going well? Keep swimming. Grad school overwhelming? Keep swimming. Car trouble? Keep swimming.

It's my go-to when I do not have a single piece of good advice to offer or if I am being real or too bogged down in "me" and my own problems to really hear and respond to what the person in front of me is saying. Some days, I am not a great friend.

A good friend would step out of themselves, strap on some goggles, grab a floatie, and swim beside them for a while. Some days, I can. Some days, I fail. I am very human. It may be time to add another sentence to that almost dismissive piece of advice though: "Keep swimming, *but* you may need to change your direction."

If we are swimming and going nowhere or, worse, miserably bobbing under the crashing waves, we will need to keep swimming. We can't go under, but maybe we do need to change our path a little.

God wants us to do more than just keep swimming. He wants us to thrive in our time here. I think He wants us to be able to see Him when we look at each other. Imagine how different our world would be if we only could.

I know when I pray asking "Lord, lead me where you want me to go," I am always slightly disappointed to find that when I open my eyes there isn't a clearly drawn out map for me! I sit there for a minute or two thinking I will hear in a Charlton Heston–type voice, "This is what I want you to do and why," so I, too, keep swimming.

The goal in swimming is to get somewhere though, right? So if all of our efforts are being put toward simply not going under, are we getting anywhere at all? God created us for His purpose, and sometimes, we simply lose our way. Let's own it and redirect.

Life is meant to be joyful and fulfilling. So if you have been swimming in what feels like an ocean during a hurricane for far too long, find some dry land and take a rest. Think about the gifts and strengths that you know God has given you. Are you using them? Or have you been so distracted and overwhelmed by life you can't even remember what it felt like to be inspired and excited about your day?

Take a rest from just swimming aimlessly to either discover or remind yourself of the gifts He has already given you. Consider all the ways that using those gifts for His glory might strengthen you for those days when we all just keep swimming.

Surround yourself with people who will support, encourage, and love you as you head in a different direction. Cherish the people who will pick up their flippers and wade in uncharted waters by your side.

Before you move from land to sea again, consider the possibility that swimming toward the life He wants for you, the one he created for you, might be a whole lot easier than swimming against the currents meant to distract us and pull us off course in this life.

Scripture reading (Jeremiah 29:11):

I will bless you with a future filled with hope—a future of success, not suffering.

Prayer~

Dear Heavenly Father,

Help me to not be distracted by all the things that keep me from you. Help me thrive in the love you freely give. Help me keep swimming toward you.

In the name of Jesus Christ, I pray, amen.

This week: ♡ ᕙ

Is there an area of your life that feels like rough waters right now? Are you stuck and not able to get where you know you need to go? Write down the distractions that are keeping you from moving forward. Own them. Then spend this week narrowing down the list so you have the energy to swim with a clearer direction.

Ladies of the Table

Photo credit: Shutterstock

Our church began a women's group called Ladies of the Table. The group was designed to be inclusive for all women both in and outside of our church family—no dues, no events to plan, no consistent structure, just time with each other in Christian fellowship. At first, it was a bit awkward. If you are at a church meeting, there is a plan, right? Then the monthly group began to morph into something all groups set as a goal, a family.

The thing is, when you don't have business and things to plan, you have time to really get to know each other. You learn about families and jobs. You learn about struggles and battles people are facing. It became, over time, that safe place to fall for women from all walks of life. We learned favorite colors and goals. We learned what makes us laugh and what makes us cry.

Women who didn't attend church regularly began to give it a try. Even those who may have never stepped in the door for worship are learning that being surrounded by women of faith can be pretty great. Much like the Las Vegas slogan, we too have a "What happens at the table, stays at the table" philosophy. It allows us to have deep and powerfully honest conversations at times that the normal structure of church meetings don't allow.

The funniest part of this story of a successful women's group? It was created by our young, single, and very male pastor. He can't even attend! He knew that women in our church needed each other in ways the current structure wasn't meeting. He is going to make some woman a great husband one day!

Scripture reading (Matthew 18:20):

Whenever two or three of you come together in my name, I am there with you.

Prayer~

Dear Heavenly Father,

Thank you for time with friends! You have taught us to accept, love, and nurture these special relationships. Help us always keep you at the head of the table as we gather.

In the name of Jesus Christ, I pray, amen.

This week: ♡ 💪

Find time for your friends! Social media friendships are not relationships. Go to lunch or out for coffee. Find time to check in with their hearts by looking them in the eye.

Who Am I?

(Photo credit: Kowshon Ye)

Have you ever looked in the mirror and wondered whose eyes were staring back? Scanning the reflection, you try to remember when the first gray hair appeared or when that wrinkle showed up on your forehead. I struggle at times with defining my life. Is one hat that I wear more important than another? Is how I make a living more important than how I make a life? Is my core, my soul, the same after years of scarring? Am I still a good person if my temper and passion make me snap and act badly?

The truth is, I am not easily defined, and that is perfectly OK. I am older, but I worked for every wrinkle and gray hair. All of my hats work together to make me who I am, and the importance of one over the other shifts. Like everyone else, I mess up badly on a regular basis. I am a great friend one day, and on others, I wonder why people claim me at all.

It's as if I struggle between who I want to be—the always kind and compassionate person and the hot mess who snaps at the drive-through lady when she hands me a half-filled cup of coffee. I have learned to cut myself some slack. I juggle switching hats and have learned the benefit and beauty each hat brings to my life. I have learned to forgive my imperfect self when I slip and react in ways that don't honor anyone, especially myself.

Most of all, I have learned not to focus all of my attention on who I am and a lot more on *whose* I am.

Scripture reading (Isaiah 49:16):

A picture of your city is drawn on my hand. You are always in my thoughts!

Prayer~

Dear Heavenly Father,

I know I am flawed, and I know that you love me anyway! Thank you! Help me as I get closer and closer to the fulfillment of your creation—who you want me to be for *your* purpose.

In the name of Jesus Christ, I pray, amen.

This week: ♡ ☙

Just be you! If you slip up, make it right and forgive yourself! Practice pausing and praying before you act.

Mattresses?

Photo credit: Shutterstock

As someone who has lived the struggles of small family-owned businesses, my all-time favorite movie scene is the "go to the mattresses" scene from the movie *You've Got Mail*. Joe Fox (owner of Fox Books chain store) gives advice to Kathleen Kelly (owner of a small family-owned bookstore) to "go to the mattresses" when her store gets in financial trouble. The quote originated from rival gangs within the Mafia and means to prepare for battle. Fox unknowingly advised the owner of the store he was trying to run out of business to fight his own efforts. She listened and prepared to go to war for her small charming bookstore. Each time she got scared, she would put on imaginary boxing gloves, put her fists up, dance around a bit, and whisper, "Go to the mattresses."

I have always been a sucker for the little guy and the underdog. I always want the good guys to win! It's so hard sometimes to get nice people in the "go the mattresses" mind-set. Too often, they believe they can't be both nice and go to battle. Most of that hesitancy comes from the realization that some people have no boundaries when they enter a fight. They don't want to get in the mud with the pigs because they don't like being dirty—the dirtier it gets, the happier the pigs become.

The thing is, we can all think of situations in our lives wherein we would like to strap on the imaginary boxing gloves and take someone out. Take a moment and select the color of your gloves! While your eyes are closed and your fists are in whatever color gloves you have chosen, dance around a bit while you think of ways to fight with your head and your heart instead of your mouth and your fists.

We don't need actual gloves to fight for principles or projects or people we believe in; we do need hearts of warriors. Keep the picture of those boxing gloves close in your mind so you can visit them from time to time. Whether it is a fight for your family, your community, your church, your business, or your health, you have the right to go to battle in a theoretical sense. It is not impolite to call someone out for unethical behavior. It is not uncivil to disagree with respect. It does not make you less faithful to passionately defend your heart in a church setting. You are not a troublemaker for defending the rights of your child in his/her school. You are not ungrateful for excellent care when you question your doctor. You are a warrior.

Being a warrior is not a bad thing. God did not create this crazy world we live in without equipping us with what we would need to battle when necessary. We just struggle knowing how to be warriors who are always grounded in love. Sometimes, we wait too long trying to get along and end up snapping.

Warriors fight for what they believe is right and just. They stand up for those who cannot stand up for themselves. They don't wear capes. Their strongest weapon is the heart. Fools go to battle over getting the wrong item in the drive-through line or having to wait five minutes for anything. Fools try to make their point by the public humiliation of another. Fools think the loudest and most obnoxious always win. I have watched many quiet faith-filled warriors take down loudmouthed giants. It is a rejuvenating thing to witness.

Don't be afraid or hesitant about strapping on the armor God gives us when needed. Be a warrior in your own life for all the things that matter. You have everything you need beating in your chest right now.

Scripture reading (Psalm 27:1)

You Lord, are the light that keeps me safe. I am not afraid of anyone. You protect me. I have no fears.

Prayer~

Dear Heavenly Father,

When I am wearing your armor into battle, make sure I am on the right side of the war. Help me to pray and listen before I step into the fray. May I be a strong and worthy warrior for all things right and true.

In the name of Jesus Christ, I pray, amen.

This week: ♡ ✍

Evaluate your life. Is there an area where you have withdrawn rather than battle for what you know to be right? Pray this week and be willing to listen for direction. You may need some gloves! Pick your color!

Meraki and the Soul Bullies

Photo credit: Shutterstock

Strolling through an open-air market nestled between the White Oak River and the Bogue Sound, we were surrounded by artists of every variety. My niece was one such artist. Marine biologist by day, she works with jellyfish at the NC Aquarium. The art that she displayed at the market fills a creative place in her soul. She was brave enough to step out and share her soul with others.

The name of her business uses the word *meraki*. Meraki is a Greek word without a clear translation, but basically, it is an adjective to describe doing something with your creativity, your love, your soul. Whatever you are creating, you are leaving a piece of yourself within it. Is there anything more courageous than sharing your soul with the world?

If I am being honest, the young women in my family are a tad bit intimidating to me. They have no fear. Between them, they have done, well, pretty much anything they have set their minds to in life so far. The word meraki describes how they live every aspect of their lives perfectly.

There will be no bucket list for these women. They surf, ride horses, play multiple instruments, create beautiful pottery, make jewelry, perform in the theater, perform with silks and hoops, paint, write powerful poetry, and do all of this and more while continuing their education and managing their careers like bosses.

They have traveled through England, France, Italy, Spain, Germany, Mexico, Costa Rica, Scotland, and they continue to add the stamps on the pages of their passports. They are fearless and intimidating in some ways, to me.

In other ways, they are inspiring. Watching them try anything and everything has made me a bit more adventurous. Seeing them fail but shake it off and keep going has made me a little more courageous. Living vicariously through them at times has made me want to open doors in my own life that I have been hesitant to walk through.

In the book *Brazen* by Leeana Tankersley, she refers to "soul bullies." They keep us from being our true selves. When we try to be brave, they bring the fear. When we feel confident enough to walk through a new door, the soul bullies bring the doubt.

Sharing this blog is walking through a new door for me. Even by stepping through it, the soul bullies still tug at me, but they are not stopping me as they have in the past. My measure of success has shifted from how other people feel about my writing to how my writing makes *me* feel. It feeds my soul.

What does your soul need? I mean, what is that piece of you that fills your soul? The gift that only God could have given you and the one He means for you to share. It may not pay the bills. It may seem silly to your ladies group. The people in the PTO might whisper about you for it, but what is that thing for you?

When fear creeps in, shut it down. When doubt steps up, keep walking through the door and shut it behind you, leaving all the fear and every bit of doubt in the dust.

God did not create us to live in fear. He doesn't want us to doubt and question the gifts He places within us. The world provides the fear and doubt. The Creator gives the strength and courage!

Scripture reading (Isaiah 41:13):

I am the Lord your God, I am holding your hand, so don't be afraid I am here to help you."

Prayer~

Dear Heavenly Father,

Take my hand, and let's walk through this door together. You created me with gifts to use for your glory! My soul is full when I use these gifts. Help me be brave!

In the name of Jesus Christ, I pray, amen.

This week: ♡ 💪

Let's all silence the soul bullies together! Think about what you do that *meraki* would describe with your heart, with your creativity, with your soul. Write it down. Remember how it felt, and then open the door and walk toward it!

Perfect Love ♡

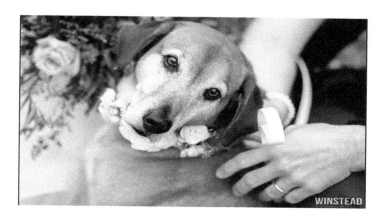

WINSTEAD

Have you ever noticed the unconditional way our dogs love us no matter what happens? Home late from work? No problem! Our dogs will be that much more happy to see us when we finally come through the door.

Our dogs don't care if we eat a pint of Ben & Jerry's Phish Food while we cry over some sappy movie. Not that I have ever done that. Our dogs will just lie beside us to snuggle and say, "We are here."

Even when we are sick and every human in the house has voluntarily quarantined themselves, our dogs have no fear! Lying on our cold feet or periodically sticking a nose in our mouths just to make sure we are still breathing—the love of our dogs is without limits.

It's no wonder dogs make such excellent emotional support and therapy animals. They seem to instinctively know what we need: when to come close, when to give us some space, when to smother us in kisses, and when to sit silently by our sides.

As imperfect humans, we struggle with what seems to come so naturally to our dogs. Sometimes, we try too hard to fix things for people we love when they really just need a safe place to vent or fall. We struggle wanting our friends and family to be happy, assuming that what brings us joy and fulfillment will be the same for them. Even in committed relationships when we have promised to love through everything, we still get hurt, and we let it show. If we are honest, we don't always quickly forgive and jump in the arms of those we love. Our dogs don't even hesitate before all is forgiven.

Don't we all just want our friends and loved ones to be like our dogs? We want them to instinctively know when to snuggle and when to bring ice cream. We expect them to instantly forgive our mistakes and outbursts and just be glad we are home!

The goal for each of us can be to care for each other with the heart of a dog.

Unconditional love and acceptance is exactly what God wants for us and that perfect love is what he gives so freely to each of us.

Scripture reading (Corinthians 16:14):

Show love in everything you do!

Prayer~

Dear Heavenly Father,

Help me to show the same unconditional love that you give to me to those around me each day. Let everything I say and every action I take begin and end with love.

In the name of Jesus Christ, I pray, amen.

This week: ♡ 💪

Who in your life gives you unconditional love? Spend some time letting them know how much that acceptance means to you.

Silence

Photo credit: Shutterstock

Every night at summer camp, we heard taps played at dusk signaling campers it was time to settle in for the night. I would sit on the stoop of the cabin, looking out over the river and wait for the last sounds of the bugle to fade before going inside.

Because of the location of my summer camp, it was not uncommon to see military aircraft in the distance as the sounds filled the night air. The sounds of freedom mixed with the sounds of loss. The innocent loss of daylight for teenagers at camp stood in stark contrast with the loss of life for those who have protected our homelands for hundreds of years. Both the aircraft and the sound of taps played at sunset serve to remind us that freedom is not, nor has it ever been, free.

There is always this haunting silence that hangs in the air for me after taps is played. I think of the wives sitting in silence with lumps in their throats as they gather themselves to go on and tears in their eyes for a husband who will never return. My mind wanders to a child waiting for one more bedtime hug that will never happen. I remember the look on the face of a father sitting in silence, waiting for his child who will not return. The silence that follows taps nearly always brings me to tears. The silence that follows the loss of any life, the absence of a love-filled laugh, a corny joke, even the absence of a familiar snore—can be deafening silence.

On Memorial Day weekend in my hometown, the local park is completely encircled with the combat boots of those who have served. Each boot has a small American flag tucked inside to remind us all what it is they are willing to lay their lives down for—our nation, yes—but for each and every one of us.

Each year, I stroll the sidewalk lined with boots in silence. It helps to remind me that for every life lost in service, there is someone, somewhere, sitting in some form of silence. I pray as I walk that each person who is left with a flag feels the love and support of a grateful nation.

Memorial Day is a time to remember and honor those lives lost in service to this amazingly complicated nation of ours. We remember the men and women who have given their lives in defense of our ability to openly debate, to freely protest, to vote without fear, and to choose our faith, our careers, our spouses.

I pray for the men and women who are currently serving as well and for their brave spouses and children who serve right beside them.

In a world where we can choose to be anything, I thank God that honorable men and women still choose to dedicate their lives in service to America. While we are on social media ripping each other to shreds over politics or the hot topic of the day, they are putting their lives on the line all around the world—for that very freedom.

Over the Memorial Day weekend, maybe we can all stand down a bit in honor of the price paid by so many. Maybe we can all take some time to be silent and thankful for every boot ever worn in service to and in defense of this messy, challenging, and glorious place we have the tremendous honor to call home.

Maybe in the silence our hearts will find a way to use the freedoms they defended with their lives to lift each other up, to build our nation up, and to honor with our daily choices the lives lost in writing this American story—an epic story by the way, which is very much a work still in progress.

Scripture reading (John 15:13):

The greatest way to show love for friends is to die for them.

Prayer~

Dear Heavenly Father,

Help me remember those who have died to secure my ability to openly and freely worship you. Thank you for this beautifully complicated country that I call home.

In the name of Jesus Christ, I pray, amen.

This week: ♡ 💪

Each day this week, send a card or note of gratitude to a service member or his/her family member. If you know a soldier who is deployed, consider sending a care package. Militaryoneclick.com can help you with all the details.

Stairs

We've all been there—standing in place considering all the options, trying to decide whether to move in one direction or another or stay put, considering whether a walk down one way would be worth the return trip. Weighing all the options, we think about all the time and energy we have invested. A walk down would require a return hike back up. We think about what has been accomplished or what is left to be done. What is down that path that we may have never even imagined?

So we stand frozen, wondering whether to take a journey with no clearly defined ending or continue to stand at the top of the stairs. As women, I think we are often prone to give more without expecting anything in return—give more to our families, to our jobs, to everyone in our lives—because somehow that defines us. But does it really? With adult daughters building their careers, I have had to redefine the message I send to them. There has to be balance. I don't want them standing at the top of the stairs scared to move. I also don't want them tumbling down. I want them bravely choosing their own direction.

There is a picture of one of mine collapsed on her laptop while we were in Greece. She did not take any time off at all last year. None. She gave 150 percent. I encouraged her to not repeat that, but there she was in arguably the most beautiful place on earth, working herself to death—passion being replaced by exhaustion.

Hard work and giving more of yourself than you get in return are admirable qualities. But, ladies, we need to take care of ourselves. I have not modeled that for my daughters. I have often given at not only my own expense, but theirs. I have stood frozen at the top of far too many staircases unable to move.

No matter where the staircase leads, it should not be a one-sided trip. Relationships, careers, service, or commitments should fill our souls in some measure as well. Or maybe it's not where our time, love, and energy need to be spent.

Life is hard, but it is also meant to be a beautiful journey full of give and take. Sometimes, a stairway is *toward* something, and other times, it is a walk away *from* something. Either way requires us to move. Time to move, ladies. Our lives are waiting!

Scripture reading (James 4:14):

What do you know about tomorrow? How can you be sure about your life? It is nothing more than mist that appears for only a little while before it disappears.

Prayer~

Dear Heavenly Father,

Help me to move! This life is too short to stand frozen worrying about what may or may not happen. Guide me to move in a direction that is pleasing to you.

In the name of Jesus Christ, I pray, amen.

This week: ♡ 💪

Move! What is at the top or bottom of the stairs in your life? Imagine what could be waiting for you if you just take that first step!

The Kitchen Crew

Photo credit: Shutterstock

Some people would consider serving 100-plus children hot meals to be work. Not the Summer Cafe crew in my hometown! Three very different women work together every week to accomplish miracles for any child who walks through our doors. They are different ages, different stages, different ethnicities, different stories of pain and loss in their lives, but they have one heart. Several of us are on the floor most days. We serve and greet and get to know our guests. We don't spend much time in the kitchen. The way I cook, that's probably a good thing!

One day, we were so busy I barely even had time to peek in and say hello, but a spill on the main floor sent me racing in the kitchen for a cleanup rag. As I came around the corner, I got a glimpse of God at work and just stopped in my tracks to breathe in the moment.

There in the middle of this crazy busy chaos, they were dancing. Laughter filled the room as they sang and clapped some silly song. They did what old people like me call the bump. They even took turns twirling each other around. The spill could wait.

So often, I have let service wear me down. This was the way I imagine God wants us to feel when we serve in His name. Complete, unadulterated joy! Serving in any capacity can be exhausting. If we lose focus, we can lose our enthusiasm and purpose. What a beautiful and clear reminder God sent me that day! Dance, sing, and serve Him—every single day.

Scripture reading (Colossians 3:23):

Do your work willingly, as though you were serving the Lord himself, and not just your earthly master.

Prayer~

Dear Heavenly Father,

Help me to always feel joy in service. Let my heart sing and dance at the thought of serving you!

In the name of Jesus Christ, I pray, amen.

This week: ♡ 💪

Find a way to bring joy to your work! Picture Christ across the table at your board meeting or sitting down for lunch at the soup kitchen. Serve every stranger as if he were Christ himself!

The Red Carpet

Photo credit: Shutterstock

Last night, I had what started out as a really great dream! I was wearing a gold glittery dress as I walked a long red carpet. Flashes were blinding me as photographers snapped away. I was smiling and waving to the crowds.

At the end of the carpet, I spot George Clooney. He is interviewing everyone as they reach the end of this walk of fame. I am so excited as I walk toward him! What will he ask me? As I get so close enough to his beautiful white teeth, that dreaming or not I believe I can smell his cologne, he leans in for what I can only imagine will be an amazing, knee-buckling hug.

This gorgeous man leans in close and whispers in my ear, "I don't know how to tell you this, but the back of your dress is stuck in your pantyhose." Cue the spinning room and cold sweat as my dream was shattered. My fading view was a panoramic shot of a million camera flashes snapping the gown stuck in my pantyhose, not to mention the horrible granny spanks. Humility lesson ruins otherwise perfect dream.

We don't all need to walk down a red carpet to feel special. Honestly, most people just need a simple acknowledgment of gratitude. Too often, we miss moments when we can notice everyday people doing really great things.

Wouldn't it be wonderful if the food pantry volunteers had a walk on that carpet? Maybe the student who organized a kindness campaign could be a star for just a moment. The custodian at your local elementary school undoubtedly deserves a spotlight moment.

One of my favorite books is *Wonder* by R. J. Palacio. I love everything about this book. It encourages us all to choose kindness. There are many quotes from the book that stay with you, but one that I love speaks to having a moment.

The main character Auggie says, "I think there should be a rule that everyone in the world should get a standing ovation at least once in their lives." I agree!

"Courage. Kindness. Friendship. Character. These are the qualities that define us as human beings, and propel us, on occasion, to greatness."

R. J. Palacio, *Wonder*

Scripture reading (Philippians 2:2–5):

Now make me completely happy! Live in harmony by showing love for each other. Be united in what you think, as if you were only one person. Don't be jealous or proud, but be humble and consider others more important than yourselves. Care about them as much as you care about yourselves and think the same way that Christ Jesus thought.

Prayer~

Dear Heavenly Father,

Thank you for all the kindness in this world! Help me to always choose kindness in my thoughts and actions. Forgive me when I fall short.

In the name of Jesus Christ, I pray, amen.

This week: ♡ ✍

I am going to challenge you, warriors (and myself), to give someone a standing ovation, a walk-down-the-carpet moment. Notice people working quietly all around you to make this world better.

Take one day to just observe the people whose lives cross paths with yours. Put the phone down and really look around you. Turn your playlist down, remove the earplugs, and listen as you walk the neighborhood.

Ordinary people are doing extraordinarily kind things all around us every single day. Let's make this the week all you heart of a warrior followers find a way to give them a moment of sincere gratitude.

The Trigger

The evening news and my social media feeds have become so negative lately it is hard not to feel like the world is falling apart. With a nudge from a friend or two, I began experimenting with mindfulness. One of the activities encouraged me to choose a gratitude trigger. I was to select something that when I saw or heard it would trigger a moment of gratitude.

I chose a plane. Why not? Living at the end of the runway for the largest Marine Corps air station would give me many moments of reflection—first and foremost, being grateful for the families who serve and sacrifice for us daily. The first week, it worked so well! I would hear the sound of freedom and pause to think of something I could be grateful for in that moment. One thing would quickly move to two, and on days of training operations, well, I might be grateful a hundred times! Imagine how grateful I was during the air show!

I never really stopped to think how many aircraft took off from that runway on any given day. Now, I catch myself counting and looking up to try and identify my trigger by name. I began to imagine their view from the air. My mind drifted to an afternoon flight over the outer banks I had taken one summer. The small Cessna flew over Cape Lookout and back toward New Bern. We flew a path that let me see from the air that amazing runway where all my gratitude triggers begin and end their journeys.

The view from above was so breathtakingly beautiful. I wonder if God looks at this earth He created and still thinks we have honored and cared for our home.

I am going to go with yes! Because in the same way we have unending faith in our children to pull it together when they mess things up, I like to think he has that faith in us.

Scripture reading (Job 37:15–16):

Can you explain why lightning flashes at the orders of God who knows all things? Or how he hangs the clouds in empty space?

Prayer~

Dear Heavenly Father,

Thank you for entrusting us with care of this beautiful earth you created for us! Help me to pause and be grateful for its majesty.
In the name of Jesus Christ, I pray, amen.

This week: ♡ ✍

Go online and explore the wonders of the world this week! Find something in your daily life that can trigger a moment of gratitude.

Waxing and Waning

Photo credit: Rachel Stringfellow

Sitting in the sand watching fiddler crabs scurry along the shore, I wait for the sun to sink below the horizon. To my left, a little sanderling follows the waves out to sea searching for dinner. To my right, an old, black Jeep Wrangler is parked just past the reach of waves as they race to the shore. Four surf fishing rods are positioned in the wet sand. A man whose skin has been blemished by the sun over time stands beside them. He peeks under the rim of his Cabela's hat with one eye toward those four poles as he casts yet another line out toward a rip current.

There is one lonely surfer well out beyond the fishing lines, and I chuckle because fools surf after 5 p.m., right? Doesn't he realize it's dinnertime for sharks?

Sunset and sunrise at the ocean are spiritual experiences for me. Beyond the absolute beauty of each setting and rising sun, I am in awe of how the sun and, particularly, the moon control the tides. I ponder the majesty of it all as the last flickers of sunlight slip away, and it is just me sitting by the sea.

In those first moments of darkness, with the ocean breeze whispering, I feel the power of my God who created this daily miracle. I must seem like a grain of sand on an endless shore to him. Yet He knows me, and He loves me.

This night, there is a full moon. I pull my old gray Camp Don Lee hoodie over my head, and I look out over the ocean. For as far as I can see, the light of the bright full moon illuminates the surface. I wonder for a moment: if I sailed a boat hundreds of miles out tonight, would I ever leave the glow cast by this moon?

In the morning, I will walk the shore as the sun rises and look for shells tossed on the shore as the tide rushes back in hours from now. I will tell myself stories of where the shell originated and how it landed here today.

Each sunset is an ending of a day, but it is also the promise of a new tomorrow. The moon will begin waning again tomorrow until it is once again a new moon.

Tides will come and go between the new and the next full moon. Fishermen will fish. Surfers will surf. Sanderlings will search for food. We will begin again, over and over. Don't miss the rest this sunset will bring so that you will be ready and able to claim the promise the sunrise will offer you to begin again tomorrow.

Scripture reading (Psalm 92:2):

It is wonderful each morning to tell about your love and at night to announce how faithful you are.

Prayer~

Dear Heavenly Father,

Thank you for the beautiful way you created this earth! Help me to praise your name as my own life waxes and wanes.

In the name of Jesus Christ, I pray, amen.

This week: ♡ 💪

Each morning as the sun rises, close your eyes and let your mind take you to nature. Write down or jot where you went each morning! Praise God for the beautiful earth he has created and given to us!

Lost

Photo credit: Shutterstock

Before GPS technology was so readily available, I set out to take one of my girls on a country day trip. Most of the day would be spent on two-lane roads with no stoplights. We were excited to explore the back roads of NC in search of a horse!

We had the best day driving through beautiful small towns. Hallmark-style streets with ice cream shops and family-owned hardware stores filled our journey, test riding a few prospects along the way. We didn't find a horse for her but had a really fun and scenic road trip.

As we began the drive home, my daughter pulled her gray hoodie over her head and fell asleep against the passenger-side car door. Shortly after, I took what we now know was a wrong turn. An hour later, my cell phone had no signal, and my gas light flashed. I was lost. All I could think about was my daughter sleeping next to me and all of the disastrous things that could happen as we continued to drive in what felt like the middle of nowhere. The adventure was no longer fun at all.

Much like the Robert Frost poem, we came to a fork in the road—no street sign, no lights. At the point where the main road separated into two choices of direction was an old country church. Only the moonlight even allowed me to see it.

Small with cracking white paint, the steeple with a small cross was nearly dead center of both roads. The church looked abandoned, but as the light hit one small stained glass window, the sight of Jesus with his outstretched hands made the abandoned building feel very much alive to me.

I pulled my car in the dirt drive, and after I wiped a few scared tears away, I prayed. I could see my husband and momentarily thought my prayer had turned to panic. Then, with no clue where either road would lead, I heard the voice of my husband telling my sleeping daughter the rules of the markers as she had prepared to take the test for her boating license, "Red, right, return home alive." Meaning when returning, keep the red marker on the right of the boat for safe passage.

I took the road on the right. Within five minutes, there was a small mom and pop gas station in front of me. The nicest man and woman were inside. They told me how to find my way home and even packed our friend chicken dinner to go.

It is hard to never lose our way in life unless we just don't ever move. GPS technology does make it a lot easier to find our actual destination!

People become lost all the time to mental illness, addictions, peer pressure—the list goes on and on. For most, we get temporarily lost. For others, life can be much like those endless dark roads for much longer periods of slow-moving time.

Thankfully, we have a road map for life in the Bible. We have an old-school compass in our prayers. For those that are lost and who wander, find a church and take that first step inside.

Most importantly, for those who are grounded today and steady on your paths, be ready to open your doors and your hearts to those who are searching for a way home.

Scripture reading (Luke 19:10)

The Son of Man came to look for and to save people who are lost.

Prayer~

Dear Heavenly Father,

Thank you for being beside me on the days I feel lost. Like a porch light left on in the dark, you always guide me home. Help others to see the way to your home through the way I live my life.

In the name of Jesus Christ, I pray, amen.

This week: ♡ ☝

Each day, write the name of one person in your life who you are worried may be lost. Pray for them. Find a way to connect with them this week to let them know you care.

Beauty in the Mess

Sometimes, life is terribly messy. Everything is going well, and then what seems like one small shift, everything changes. Trust might be lost due to a betrayal. Faith in a person you admire might be tainted when a character flaw rears its ugly head. Your motivation to change the world goes up in flames because what you believed and who you believed in is just done. You work hard. You give your best. You are honest and dependable. You are uncompromising in your beliefs. Yet all around you, people are being celebrated and acknowledged who exemplify all the characteristics you work hard to not embrace.

Suddenly, it's messy and complicated and confusing. You wonder how in the world you will get motivated when you feel unappreciated. You wonder how you will trust again when you have been betrayed. You wonder if you will ever feel inspired again when your inspiration now sucks the life out of you.

How on earth will you turn it around, not for them, but for you? How on earth indeed.

In Iceland, there is a place where you can snorkel and scuba dive in fissures created by earthquakes. Absolutely clear glacier water allows you to see the power created as the tectonic plates between the North American and the Eurasian plates shift. The plates shift, earthquakes happen to release pressure and, in the process, something of glorious beauty and majesty is created.

The Greek island of Santorini is part of a Caldera. Before 1646 BC, the island was named Thera. In 1646 BC, the largest volcanic eruption known to man resulted in a collapse of Thera. Santorini is the circular part remaining of Thera that rises above the Aegean Sea. The resulting caldera leaves most of the original island submerged. Many believe the massive eruption and resulting tsunamis lead to the end of the Minoan civilization. Yet today, the island of Santorini and the caldera that resulted draw millions for its majestic beauty and what some believe are healing waters.

Maybe we do need to look at the earth to see how disasters in our lives can create beautiful opportunities. Is it possible to find beauty after destruction? The handiwork of God with our world suggests yes. It may be hard to see how anything beautiful can possibly follow mild, shifting quakes in your life or major destructive eruptions, but God is a mighty God! Overcoming the destruction in our lives and being able to open our hearts to the possibility of beauty can bring unfathomable restoration.

Scripture reading (Psalm 71:20–21)

You made me suffer a lot, but you will bring me back from this deep pit and give me new life. You will make me truly great and take my sorrow away.

Prayer~

Dear Heavenly Father,

Just as you bring renewal to the earth, help me find renewed strength for the challenges ahead. Thank you for surrounding me with reminders that great beauty can follow great destruction.

In the name of Jesus Christ, I pray, amen.

This week: ♡ 💪

Do some research on the history of our earth. Find times when great beauty followed destruction. Screenshot a picture, and place it with this devotion or in your Bible. It can serve as a reminder that renewal is possible.

Pink Flamingo

Photo credit: Shutterstock

The other night, I had the most joy-filled dream! My mother, who died last year after a struggle with Alzheimer's, was racing in a pool riding a giant inflatable pink flamingo. She had that red tint back in her hair. She was laughing that full amazing laugh she had before the disease confused her. Water was splashing everywhere as the giant pink flamingo pulled her down one lane of an Olympic-size swimming pool.

The best part of the dream was that she was waving and smiling at the crowds in the stands as if she were Miss America. When she raced by me as I stood along the fence, her eyes locked with mine, and her Miss America wave turned to her signature—one finger at a time, starting with the pinky—flowing wave as she shouted, "Look at me!"

The thing is, since my mother died, my memories have been clouded by effects the disease took on her mind and body. Even the dreams I can remember have been of her during the long goodbye.

Not that night! I could hear her laugh. I could see that glint in her eye when she smiled. I could feel her all around me.

Replaying the day and trying to figure out why my pink flamingo riding mom showed up tonight, it had been filled with goodbyes. One of my dear friends was hurting as her father slipped away. One of my daughters was moving away, and even though I was happy, I was struggling a bit too.

So maybe the dream was a way to remind me that goodbye is not forever. It's for now. Maybe in some weird way that pink flamingo is now a trigger for me to know that happiness can follow the goodbyes in our lives. Maybe it was the white chocolate mocha I had before bedtime.

Either way, it was a turning point in my grieving process. Just as in all the turning points of my life, my mother was right there smiling.

Scripture reading (Matthew 5:4):

God blesses those people who grieve. They will find comfort!

Prayer~

Dear Heavenly Father,

Thank you for memories of those who we have loved and lost. Thanks for reminders of all sorts that goodbye is not forever but for now.

In the name of Jesus Christ, I pray, amen.

This week: ♡ 💪

Each morning, spend time remembering moments with someone you have lost. Write the memory down so you can revisit it later.

Disguises

Photo credit: Shutterstock

One of my favorite stories is from a pastor visiting the new church where he would be assigned. None of the congregation had met him or knew what he looked like. He entered and sat in the back of the sanctuary. He was not dressed as a traditional pastor. His tattoos showed beneath his short-sleeved shirt.

Not one person greeted him the entire morning. The next week, when he was introduced as the new pastor in more traditional attire, they didn't even remember him, but he remembered how they made him feel. He wasn't even in disguise.

Yet so many of us walk around wearing masks of some sort. Women, especially, have been trained to get up, dress up, and show up no matter how we feel. So we do. Anything less feels like weakness.

Recently, I had dinner with a friend. If we are honest, we wear masks all the time. The two of us are silly enough to think God can't see us. Each of us set the bar so high for ourselves that even the slightest slip feels like failure. Be strong. Do it all. Be everything for everyone. You all know the drill! We all think we are wonder women or that we should be wonder women.

We couldn't even cancel a dinner date when we each would have been justified to stay home. We could have locked ourselves in our bathrooms while we took an hour-long bubble bath with a box of chocolate close by our sides and just cried those long therapeutic cries we all need. Instead, we got up, we semi-dressed up (a.k.a. we put clothes that were not pajamas on), and we showed up.

We sat together in a back corner booth and took turns crying in a crowded Mexican restaurant for two hours. We laughed a lot too in-between the tears. But we showed up! We showed up for each other when we were not able to put the masks on for the world. Our poor waitress...

You know who else showed up? God. He knows us without our disguises. He knows us and loves us anyway.

What a different world it would be today if we all just accepted that we are already *enough*. Crying in our bubble baths while we eat chocolate, we are enough. Being able to say no without guilt, we are enough. Not being able to fix everything, we are enough. The best part? God is enough, so put the disguises away and show up for this day as just you. The amazingly imperfect and loved beyond measure—*you*.

Scripture reading (Romans 8:38–39):

I am sure that nothing can separate us from God's love—not life or death, not angels or spirits, not the present or the future, and not powers above or powers below. Nothing in all creation can separate us from God's love for us in Christ Jesus our Lord!

Prayer~

Dear Heavenly Father,

Thank you for creating me with everything I need to live a life that honors you! Thank you for reminding me that I am enough for you!

In the name of Jesus Christ, I pray, amen.

This week: ♡ 💪

Each day, begin with I am enough. At the end of the day, before you close your eyes, write down one thing that went really well. Write beside it: I am enough.

The Stories We Tell

Photo credit: Shutterstock

We are all really creative people! Think about it. Over the course of our lives, we tell ourselves so many stories as coping mechanisms or personal sabotage. It's like our own version of inaccurate news playing nonstop in our heads.

The story: my new neighbor doesn't like me. She thinks I am strange or boring. The reality: her marriage is falling apart, and she is trying to hide it from the world. So she avoids me or cuts conversations short.

In one version, I am not good enough for that job. I have given twenty years of my life, and it has been wasted. The reality, my boss knows the perfect fit for me is a promotion right around the corner. I am needed more for that position. I am more than enough. My story versus the reality makes me do something not very smart.

One chapter reads, "Man, that woman is wound tight as a top! She is such a snob." The truth—her life is completely out of control. So she is holding tight and controlling the situations in her life in which she can guarantee the outcomes. She is actually a lot like you and would make a great friend.

We all do it! We write very imaginative tales in our heads every single day: why someone cuts us off at the light, why someone isn't working, why someone is just plain rude. The most dangerous stories we write are about ourselves.

I am not good enough. I am too good. I am not strong enough. I am too strong. I am not pretty enough. I am too pretty (said no woman ever). I am too loud. I am too quiet. I am too abrupt. I am a marshmallow. I am too honest. I sugarcoat everything. I am too nice. I am not nice enough. I am not smart enough. I am too smart.

On and on we go.

We tell ourselves we can't find the time to travel when we are terrified of flying. We tell ourselves we like being alone when we are too frightened of ever letting someone close enough to shred our hearts into tiny pieces again.

Anything sound familiar? The thing is, the stories we tell ourselves keep us from the truest version God is trying to help us write for our lives. We let our imaginations cloud the beautiful reality.

All the dragons and witches from childhood fairy tales creep in on us, and their noise in our heads crowd out the true author of our life stories. Quiet the villains in your head. Let the epic version of your life unfold.

Scripture reading (Job 31:19):

After all, God is the one who gave life to each of us before we were born.

Prayer~

Dear Heavenly Father,

Help me to be still and hear the stories you have planned for my life. Help me crowd out the noise so that we can begin to write the story you imagine for me!

In the name of Jesus Christ, I pray, amen.

This week: ♡ 💪

Each morning, write one dream you had for yourself as a child. Spend the day remembering what happened to that dream.

Backpack

Photo credit: Kowshen Ye

We could hear the beautiful melody of a John Legend song coming from the piano in the choir room. It was strange that in the middle of a packed house for our summer feeding program, the choir would practice. Stranger still, they were practicing with a John Legend song!

Opening the door, we stopped and just stared. Inside was a young man who had been a regular in our program this summer. As we began to talk to him, we discovered his passion for music. He loved playing the piano and guitar. He wanted to learn the violin. The only opportunity he had to do either was when he entered our church doors and would sneak down to the sanctuary or choir room. Not going to lie, we were all choking back tears.

He was nineteen. He struggled with social and verbal skills. He was quite possibly autistic. He was clearly gifted. We all began to visit him one-on-one trying to piece together how this gift had never been shared and cultivated. Working with children and families who live in poverty, you learn quickly that their day-to-day survival takes precedence over long-term planning.

Standing in the hallway, several women from our church did not want this day to be added to the list of missed opportunities for his life. Our program was ending. Our support and love have no time limit. Within an hour, one of our church members delivered a keyboard he could take home and play all day any day.

Other children received their backpacks from the summer program that day. They spoke of favorite subjects and teachers. Each backpack had their grade-specific list of supplies, books selected just for them, and a handwritten note of hope and love from the congregation. He took home a keyboard and the biggest smile that words cannot describe. At least I cannot find the words to describe his smile, but I will never forget it.

I couldn't help but wonder what gifts were being missed in every single child who received a backpack that day. Would his life be different today had someone noticed earlier that he loved music so much? Would he be in a different place had someone advocated for him to be in the fine arts classes? He had never taken a music course of any kind, trust me; it would have only taken one class for someone to notice his talent.

We, as a society, often try to put students in boxes. We think they all need to learn at the same speed. They all need to mature at the same pace. They all need to respond the same way even if their life experiences are polar opposites. Do they? Or are we stifling the very gifts God intended for them to share with the world?

Teachers know better. Look at the picture in this blog. It's a high school teacher hugging one of her students. The love shows. I can only imagine what a teacher would need in his/her backpack to meet the unique and growing needs of every child. One thing I know for sure, they need us. They need warriors. ♡ ⓑ

Giving this child backpacks year after year probably would not have helped him. I am sure it would have cultivated a trusting relationship with our church family. Imagine though if his gift with and passion for music had been discovered in, say, sixth grade. He would have been exposed to a whole world of opportunities that could have helped to strengthen him in so many other areas. His school experience would have been or could have been very different. It's never too late, and he will always have a place to practice now!

Backpacks are wonderful things! Wouldn't it be amazing if when we prayed over them, we could see clearly and exactly what that specific child really needed packed in order to have a successful and happy school year?

Close your eyes. Picture this young man sitting at a piano in your empty sanctuary. His jeans are tattered. His T-shirt is too large and stained. His sneakers are being held together by threads. Yet he is beautifully sitting at your piano with the sun glistening through a stained glass window and bouncing off his fingers as he plays.

Let your heart hear the music he is playing. Whether it's John Legend or John Wesley, close your eyes and listen as he plays with passion, notes he cannot read. Listen as he teaches you how to feel the music.

Know that in your community, there are children just like him all around you. Open your hearts. Open your doors. Let them in. Don't miss the opportunity to fill a backpack with love, support, and acceptance.

Scripture reading (Matthew 18:5):

And when you welcome one of these children because of me, you welcome me.

Prayer~

Dear Heavenly Father,

Help me to be open to helping those in need. Open my eyes to see the children living in poverty all around me each day. Help me find a way to serve as your hands and feet in making their lives better here.

In the name of Jesus Christ, I pray, amen.

This week: ♡ 💪

Explore the ways your community serves children living in poverty. Find a way to help.

Closets

Photo credit: Shutterstock

Cleaning out closets should happen more than every ten years, but better late than never! It was actually a fun way to spend the afternoon with one of my daughters. She does need to give her husband some closet space after all.

Putting the clothes in piles for Goodwill, we would pause on special outfits and reminisce a little about the event where this particular outfit made its debut appearance—dresses from dances, T-shirts from student council conventions, jackets from her first job, hoodies from each and every day of her life apparently.

About halfway through one of the hoodie boxes, she paused. She looked at the old, gray band sweatshirt from her trombone section, ran her fingers across one of the names, and cried. I knew watching her, the memories of his crazy great laugh were replaying in her head.

She was remembering his ear to ear smile. She was mourning a life lost too soon.

Older now and more battle-weary herself, there was also an understanding and empathy for the very real struggles so many people face every single day. Tears were being shed for the loss of that innocence they shared all those years ago on a high school band field.

When we were young, we thought we were invincible. We drove too fast. We stayed in the sun all day. We tossed friendships to the side because we thought there would always be plenty of time for making up later. We were so wrong.

Each and every one of us have names—people from our youth whose loss shook us forcefully into the reality that this is a temporary home we share. Their faces are forever in our hearts because aside from all the joy they brought to our lives, their loss made us value and measure our own time and our moments in a new way.

This life is short. The journey seems easy for some and extremely difficult for others. The truth is, it's hard for everyone, just in different ways and at different times perhaps. The exposed surfaces of our lives are often covering crippling pain.

The thing is that in-between the moments of pain and sorrow are tremendous capsules of time filled with so much laughter, love, and joy. We need to balance and learn from both extremes.

We keep the memories of every bit of it—the good, the bad, and the ugly—in the closets of our lives as if pulling it out will ruin a good thing. Actually pulling it all out, owning every piece of it as what has made us who we are, letting go of some of it, and holding on to the best parts might be the best way to find that balance.

Scripture reading (John 3:16):

God loved the people of this world so much that he gave his only Son, so that everyone who has faith in him will have eternal life and never really die.

Prayer~

Dear Heavenly Father,

Help me to have empathy for those who struggle with loss. Strengthen me to support and love them through the pain.

In the name of Jesus Christ, I pray, amen.

This week: ♡ 💪

Do some research on depression. Learn what the warning signs are of someone struggling with clinical depression. Find out how you can help.

Walk, Run, Sail

Photo credit: Shutterstock

Have you ever wanted to run—not walk away from something? When I was six, I ran away for about thirty minutes. It was cleaning day, and I did not want to do my chores. I left the yard and hid behind a gardenia bush at the edge of the woods by our house. The sound of my mother calling the first time made me think, *She will make me cookies when she finds me.* When I heard her call my name again with a different tone, I just ran home. I was scared, and I wanted my mommy.

In college when it felt like the world was closing in, I filled my candy apple red Jetta up with gas, put my Pretenders cassette tape in, and drove all night with no plan. When the sun came up, I was somewhere in South Carolina. No GPS and no cell phone, I had to stop at a gas station and get an old-fashioned paper map to find my way back.

Grownup a.k.a. old me sometimes wants to launch a sailboat to anywhere there are blue skies and calm waters. Remember the Styx song, "Come Sail Away"? It is on repeat in my head on those days.

As with everyone, life gets hectic and jumbled up, especially when we overcommit ourselves. It feels like everyone is asking me, "What are you going to do about it?" In my head, I am already imagining the sailboat as the music begins to play. I ponder how the words "absolutely nothing" being spoken as I walk away would go over as a response.

Recently, I was somewhere thinking I was being helpful, but it felt like obligation, not joyful service. People were arguing over something that seemed so ridiculous to me. Indignation began my thought process. "Good Lord, look around! We have big problems, and we are going to argue all night over this?" I am sure it was important to them, but did I really need to be there?

Is this where God needed me to serve? Was my voice needed in this discussion? Was this an area my heart could help, or was it an area that would harden my heart in spots? My eyes glazed over, the sailboat was approaching. But just as the music began to play, I felt the words "I want so much more for you than this" run throughout every cell in my body. Less frustration, more joy. Less quibbling, more love. Less saying yes to them; more saying yes to me. I need to work on letting His presence drown out the noise more often.

Serving God doesn't mean running ourselves to death and never saying no. Old me thinks it is about less whining and more listening. People can't hear God in my voice if I am whining. They can't see Him in me if I am not serving in ways that honor Him. Old me thinks I need to be more intentional about my time and spend more of it sailing toward the areas where God wants me working—for whatever purpose He has in store.

How about you? Are you wanting to walk, run, or sail away from some things in your life? Or are you ready to move toward something wonderful?

Scripture reading (2 Chronicles 15:7):

So you must be brave. Don't give up! God will honor you for obeying him.

Prayer~

Dear Heavenly Father,

Help me to understand where you want me to serve. Then give me the strength and courage to not give up!
In the name of Jesus Christ, I pray, amen.

This week: ♡ ✍

Make a list of all of your obligations. Which ones bring you joy? Which ones do you feel called to serve in some capacity? Pray over each one and listen to hear God.

No Fear

We love to ride around in our little boat in the evenings. One day last week as we rounded the corner to our house, I noticed a deer on the bank. She was so close I could have touched her. There was no fear. No need to hide. It's as if she knew the guy driving the boat was the same man who threw deer corn out for her every night. She knew she would not be harmed.

How beautiful she was, standing free in her own habitat without fear and just watching us. I will admit that we both worried for her that close to the water because the alligators living in that creek seem to like deer.

I couldn't help but wonder how peaceful our own lives would be if we could recognize the one who "feeds" us when we are alone in the wilderness. We get lost and confused sometimes, and God our Father who gives us everything we need is right in front of us. Yet, we often can't recognize Him in the chaos.

Like my husband throwing corn out for the deer, God is surrounding us with what we need to thrive. We are not always as confident as the deer. We hide and wait for proof that we are safe, proof that we can trust, proof that He is who He says He is.

What if just for today, we walked through life watching for and recognizing God all around us? Could we close our eyes and feel Him in the gentle breeze? Would we be able to listen for Him in the voices of strangers? Would we see Him even in the crazy wilderness we find ourselves?

Let's try it!

Scripture reading (John 5:37):

The Father who sent me also speaks for me, but you have never heard his voice or seen him face to face.

Prayer~

Dear Heavenly Father,

Help me to see you when you are right in front of me! Help me to feel your presence, and let it strengthen me when I am afraid.
In the name of Jesus Christ, I pray, amen.

This week: ♡ 💪

Consider the times in your life when you felt lost and alone. Really reflect. Was there someone with you? Looking back from where you are now in life, can you see where God was with you?

About the Author

Kim Rice Smith is the author of the Christian Facebook blog, *The Heart of a Warrior*. Kim has often been referred to as a warrior for children. Although that nickname sparked the blog title, she considers all women to be the inspiration for the blog.

Kim recognizes all women are warriors for their families, their local schools, their communities, their churches, and everything their hearts can hold. Warriors need faith. Warriors need each other. For nearly a decade, Kim wrote a column for her community paper, sharing her heart with other parents. In 2006, she was awarded by the NC Press Association for her contributions in the serious columns category.

Her entire adult life has been spent serving children through service in her local and district level United Methodist Church, her community, and her local school board.

In 2014, the NC Conference of the United Methodist Church recognized her with the Saints of God Stewardship Award for her service to children living in poverty. She currently serves as the coordinator for the Sound District of NC Congregations 4 Children committee which works to build partnerships between public schools and the faith-based communities.

Kim lives in NC with her husband Larry and their dog Daisy. She has raised two daughters who she considers strong warriors, intent on making this world a better place.

You are invited to follow her blog at https://www.facebook.com/TheHeartOfAWarrior65/